Utah!

A Family Travel Guide

A complete guide to
Utah's deserts, mountains
and cities with an emphasis on car
camping, short hikes and other
outdoor activities.

To Gayen —

    who introduced me

        to Utah's wild places,

    and gave me four wonderful children

        to enjoy them with.

Canada Geese

Utah!
A Family Travel Guide

by
Tom Wharton

Photography by Dan Miller
Illustrations by Steve Baker

Wasatch Publishers, Inc.
Salt Lake City, Utah
1987

Copyright © 1987
Wasatch Publishers, Inc.
4647 Idlewild Road
Salt Lake City, Utah 84124
ISBN: 0-915272-31-8
Second Printing 1988

ACKNOWLEDGMENTS

There is more to visiting Utah than just seeing spectacular scenery. This is a state where people care about helping one another. There have been countless times when the kind words of a park ranger, the advice of a waitress in a small-town cafe or the help provided by a stranger in an out-of-the-way garage have turned an ordinary trip into something special. The people who work and enjoy Utah's parks and recreation areas are more than folks just doing their job. They are friends.

These friends spent hours helping produce this book.

Friends like Bob Donohoe, Jack Schroeder and Mary Shelsby volunteered to help edit. Relatives like Jack, Vi and Lori Wharton and Harvey and Esther Gustaveson checked the manuscript when they would have rather been golfing or fishing. Folks like Zion's Victor Jackson; Bryce Canyon's Margaret Littlejohn; Canyonlands Jerry Rumburg; Arches' Anna Marie Fender and Capitol Reef's Bryce Babcock; the Utah Division of Parks and Recreation's Kay Boulter and Gordon Tenney; the U.S. Forest Service's Kathy Pollock, Barry Wirth and Ann Matjeko; the National Park Service's Don Gillespie, and the Bureau of Land Management's Jack Reed took time from their busy schedules to provide valuable information and review the text for accuracy. There were dozens of state park super-intendents, museum workers, amusement park owners and national monument interpreters who provided information on how families could enjoy their areas.

Photographer Dan Miller and artist Steve Baker were casual acquaintances before this project was started. I now consider them close friends. The hours they spent traveling Utah for inspiration and then laboring over their work went far and above what was expected. Their excellent work shows great pride and care.

Publisher Mel Davis proved to be a friend as well. He was willing to take a chance on publishing my first book and was quick to return a phone call or meet with us to offer advice.

It would have been difficult to complete this book if it hadn't been for the support of my employer, *The Salt Lake Tribune*. In the 11 years that I have been outdoor editor of that newspaper, I have been allowed to explore and write about nearly every part of Utah. For this I am grateful.

Then, there was my wife Gayen. More than any one person, she was the inspiration behind the words. She introduced me to quiet sunsets in isolated deserts, the Wasatch Mountains after a heavy winter storm, a red rock canyon bathed in golden fall colors and Easter vacations in all kinds of weather. She edited and retyped manuscripts. She pleaded with me to write feelings and not just words.

More important than that, Gayen gave me Emma, Rawl, Jacob and Bryer who have allowed me to explore Utah through their eyes. Their laughter, sense of adventure and love of the outdoors makes them more than hiking companions. My four children have given me nights when the wind "sounded like a secret," shouts of joy when they have seen a place that looked like "miles and miles of fun" and simple laughter. For these things, I am grateful.

Tom Wharton

Kids Tubing

Contents

Kids on Slickrock

INTRODUCTION

It Sounds Like a Secret

The blazing summer sun turned the inside of the automobile into a furnace as we drove south from our Salt Lake City home. The kids were screaming at each other in the back seat and my arm ached from having spent the morning loading the family car with suitcases and camping equipment.

"Are we there yet, Daddy?" screamed the kids. Again. Again. And again.

The tension mounted, along with the traffic, and I started to wonder: "Is it worth it?"

The campground at Arches National Park was full, so we checked into a small motel in nearby Moab. It was too early in the afternoon to eat dinner.

Arches National Park was just four miles away. Perhaps a quick drive and a short hike would finally calm my excited children. It was time to have some fun.

As we hit the entrance to the park something changed. The children's imaginations started to run wild. My wife told them to look at the unusual red rock formations and see if they didn't look like something else.

"Those look like penguins!" shouted four-year-old Emma.

"That one looks like a bird!" screamed Rawl, a twin 18 months younger than their sister.

"A camel! A camel! I see a camel!" shouted Jacob, the other twin as he picked up the enthusiasm.

By this time it was almost dusk and the west side of the park glowed a brilliant red. The Fiery Furnace appeared as if it were a mass of glowing embers.

Only one car remained at the trailhead. With young children it is wise to plan short hikes. Our destination this evening would be two beautiful arches just a few short blocks from the parking lot.

The kids exploded from the car, anxious to start exploring. The twins, still in diapers, waddled down the sandy trail, stopping now and again to play in the sand. Emma was singing softly.

It wasn't long before the other people on the trail finished their hike and drove away. Suddenly, we had our own corner of Arches to ourselves.

Jacob heard an echo for the first time. It happened quite by accident. He had started screaming at his sister and, much to his surprise, his wails bounced off the nearby sandstone walls. This was an experience he wasn't quite certain how to deal with. He ran to his mother's side.

It was getting dark now and the wind whipped through the box canyon, creating nature's own symphony. The kids, a bit frightened at the prospect of being alone in this strange setting, started clinging to our hands. Their eyes were wide with wonder and their ears sensitive to sound as they saw and heard things in ways they had never dreamed of before.

"What is that you hear?" my wife asked Emma softly.

My daughter listened intently. She had a simple and direct reply.

"It sounds like a secret," she whispered.

The wind sounded like a secret. Only it knew what secrets this national park and dozens of spots in Utah just like it might hold for a family. Only it knew the secret of unlocking a child's imagination. Only the wind knew how an ordinary evening suddenly was transformed into an unforgettable experience. A secret? Yes.

Traveling with the kids that day had been a hassle. There had been dirty diapers, temper tantrums, expensive meals, forgotten security blankets and angry exchanges. There had been more than a few times when we'd seriously contemplated turning back.

But, as our family sat in a lonely corner of the world with nothing to entertain us but some ancient rocks and our own imaginations, we had been transformed. Traveling wasn't such a hassle after all.

It was almost dark now. The sun had set and all that remained of daylight was a thin band of dark orange at the tops of the distant mountain range.

Slowly, the eastern sky started to light up. First seen peaking through a nearby arch, a full moon bathed Arches National Park. The kids had seen full moons before, but none like this. Their fright disappeared. The sounds of young voices could be heard singing an old folk song. "Someone's happy, Lord, kumbaya. Someone's happy, Lord, kumbaya. Someone's happy, Lord, kumbaya. Oh, Lord, kumbaya. Someone's peaceful, Lord. . . . "

Songs were sung on the way back to Moab in the shortest, most joyful journey I could ever remember. At the local pizza parlor, the magic remained. We just didn't want to let go of the feelings.

I think about that night in Arches often as friends ask me why my family spends so many vacations near home in Utah. When they do, I think about playing with the Frisbee under a full moon at Goblin Valley State Park. I remember our first family backpacking trip in the High Uintas.

There was the discovery of seeing the dinosaur quarry at Dinosaur National Monument and the looks of wonder on my kids' faces as they toured Timpanogos Cave.

I remember times when our trips became more exciting than we had bargained for. There was the night it snowed on us at Canyonlands. There was the fear of being caught in a tiny boat at Lake Powell as a storm blew over us. There was the evening the car stalled on the hot, dusty Burr Trail.

Yet, what hidden value is there in the growing imagination of a young girl as she discovers a piece of ancient Indian pottery on a hike at Edge of the Cedars State Park? What does it do for a young boy's self-image as he finishes his first hike to a high, Utah mountain lake? And, what can a father learn from his children as they force him to slow down and view nature on their terms?

Only the wind knows the answers to all the secrets that a family vacation in Utah can unveil. But some things are certain. Trips that stimulate a child's imagination can increase his interest in natural science, help him learn about history and teach him to trust in his own skills. They can help him grow into a well-rounded, thoughtful, and confident individual.

It may seem easier to sit home watching television or to leave the kids home with a babysitter while you enjoy a vacation.

Yet, the special moments more than make up for the disasters. For every whining, tired child, there is a lesson out there to be learned. For every dirty diaper to change in worn out roadside restrooms, there is a night of roasting marshmallows and singing old songs around the campfire. For every overheated radiator, there are dozens of experiences where a child and his parents can deepen their relationship. For every long, disastrous drive across the desert, there is that one night at Arches, where the wind sounds like a secret.

It Sounds Like a Secret

11

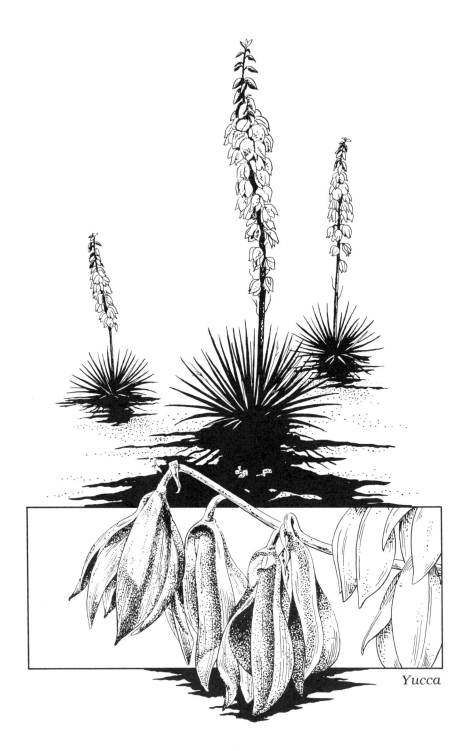

Yucca

CHAPTER ONE

National Parks

A six-year-old boy examined the campground at Arches National Park with a knowing eye. He looked at the fine coral sand, the nearby red sandstone walls, the animal tracks in the mud and the arch guarding the campfire circle.

As he reached out towards this natural playground with all the enthusiasm he could muster, he exclaimed with a shout, "Wow! Miles and miles of fun!"

There is no better way to describe a child's reaction to one of Utah's five national parks. Arches, Bryce Canyon, Canyonlands, Capitol Reef and Zion National Parks are all unique and magical places for children.

The National Park Service goes out of its way to make a child's visit out of the ordinary. Visitor centers have displays of leaves, animal tracks and rocks. On guided walks, rangers delight in giving instruction to young children. It is a rare park that doesn't offer short, guided nature trails to introduce the very young hiker to the outdoors.

Utah's national parks are similar in many respects. All feature spectacular views of desert red rock country. All are most crowded during the summer months, when school is out and tourists from all over the country are visiting. All have campgrounds open year-round and feature interpretive programs and self-guided hikes. No advance reservations are taken at the park campgrounds, though nearby Utah state parks and private facilities offer that service.

The first question most parents ask about Utah's national parks is, "When is the best time to visit them?" That isn't an easy question to answer, largely because there are different things to see during different seasons of the year. A child taking a snowshoe trip to the bottom of Bryce Canyon in the middle of the winter is going to come away with a much different feeling than one who shares the trail with hundreds of tourists on a hot July afternoon. A little girl who loves wildflowers might be enchanted with a visit to Arches' Courthouse Wash in the spring while a young boy who would enjoy taking this hike with a ranger isn't often going to have a chance to during the winter, when Utah's parks operate with small staffs and offer few interpretive programs.

There is something unique about each season. Spring and fall are good times to visit Utah's national parks because the weather is cooler. The advantage of a summer trip is that all interpretive activities are underway. During the summer months, the parks offer campfire programs and guided hikes geared toward children. Activities furnished by commercial outfitters like horseback riding, river running, four-wheel drive trips and in-park lodging are also available. Winter trips can be difficult and give visitors the chance to experience solitude. The best recommendation is to try taking trips during all four seasons. If you prepare for the weather, your kids will enjoy visiting a park just about any time of year.

If you plan on camping at a Utah national park, a word of caution is in order. Get there early! The campgrounds at Arches, Canyonlands (Squaw Flat) and Capitol Reef are relatively small and, from March until late October, often fill by the middle of the day. The facilities at Bryce Canyon and Zion, though much larger, can also fill during the busy summer tourist season. If you think a national park campground might be full, make certain there is a private or state park facility nearby. Plan ahead. There is nothing worse than traveling all day in a hot car with kids who are anxious to discover the joys of a national park, only to find there is no place to camp.

While all five parks are similar in some respects, they offer different recreational experiences that your children won't soon forget.

Here is a park-by-park look at Utah's national parks and what they have to offer:

Arches

The minute you make the five-mile drive from Moab into Arches National Park, you will sense a certain feeling in the air. It is something that says "this is someplace special," full of nooks and crannies to explore, secrets in sandstone to unlock and old friends to rediscover. In dozens of visits to Arches, the butterflies in my stomach and the many memories that flood back from past family vacations fill me with anticipation.

Perhaps, it is the thrill of seeing the Delicate Arch. Or, maybe it is the chance to see water flowing off the red sandstone in waterfalls under the Double Arch in a driving rainstorm. It might be the fun the kids have shouting with glee as they rename rock formations to suit their own imaginations.

Arches is an easy national park to enjoy with your children because of its short hikes, scenic campground and interpretive programs. There are no in-park lodging facilities at Arches, though the town of Moab, five miles from the park entrance, has plenty of lodging. If you plan to camp at Arches, you would do well to drive through the entire park to the campground, which is located at the end of the paved road. There are only 53 sites here, so get to the campground early in the day if you want to stay in the park. Don't waste the drive the campground, either. Point out the balanced rocks and other unusual rock formations you'll see on the way. My children delight in naming the different rocks. This one is a penguin and that one an elephant.

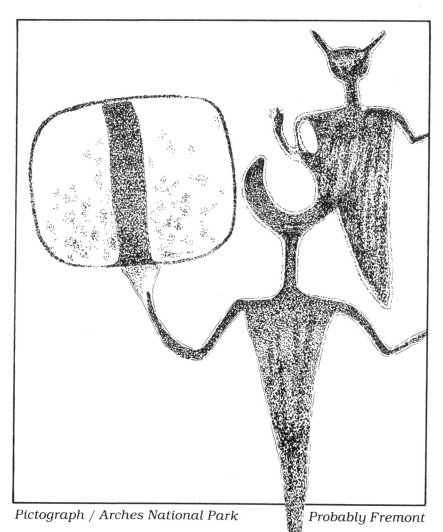

Pictograph / Arches National Park   *Probably Fremont*

You can start learning about Arches by taking the short, self-guided **Desert Nature Trail**, located near the park's visitor center at the entrance. It is only one-fifth mile and will help your child learn the names of many of the plants he'll see in this desert country. My wife has a theory that, if a child knows the name of something, that thing will become his friend. This is a good place to begin making friends with Arches National Park. It is no accident that the word "yucca," the name of a common desert plant seen at Arches, was one of the first words ever spoken by my four children. They delighted in screaming "Yucca! Yucca! Yucca!" every time they saw one of these plants.

After setting up camp, one of the first hikes you might consider taking with your children is the **Sand Dune Arch Trail**, located one mile south of the campground. The trail to this little arch is only one-fifth mile and is level and easy for children to negotiate. There is much to see in that short walk. First, the arch itself is hidden, which helps build a little suspense. Second, because the trail is in a narrow, slickrock crevice, it will appear to be going nowhere. The trail will take you through a passage barely wide enough for a person's shoulders with walls going up either side. At the end, **Sand Dune Arch** is hidden in a small canyon. Underneath the arch is a large sand dune. Young children can spend half a day at the Sand Dune Arch, playing in the sand, rolling down the dune and trying to hike up the slightly steep incline to get directly under the arch. This is a fine place to sit and relax while watching the kids play.

The next part of Arches you might consider traveling to is the **Windows Section**. Again, the hikes here are short. A personal favorite is the one-fourth mile hike to **Double Arch**, a magnificent pair of arches eroded from one common base. As you get to within about a city-block of the arches on this easy walk, shout out one of your children's names. There is an echo here. For my kids, this was their first experience with echoes. On one occasion, we heard a man sitting under one of the arches playing a flute. The sound of the instrument filled the rocky ledges with haunting melodies.

Another short trail in this area leads around the **Balanced Rock**. Families who have enjoyed the runaway train ride at Disneyland can see what a real "balanced rock" looks like. There is also a .9-mile round trip hike to **North** and **South Window** and **Turret Arch**. As you stand near these windows, look out over the rest of Arches and search for other windows and arches.

During the spring, summer and fall (roughly March to September), naturalist programs are conducted at Arches. Most kids love to take a guided hike with a ranger. Naturalist-guided hikes at Arches can often include wildflower walks, an examination of quicksand in **Court House Wash** in the spring (the kids love this one!) or the most strenuous guided hike, the two-mile trek through the **Fiery Furnace**. This guided hike is offered on the most regular basis at Arches. Ranger-led walks explore a

Swinging Bridge at Arches

labyrinth of sandstone passageways called fins. Young children can take this hike (my twin sons were three and secured with harnesses when we first attempted it) but some caution is advised.

For a slightly longer family hike, try the one-mile **Park Avenue Trail**. This is especially easy if you are hiking with friends and can put one vehicle on each end of the trailhead. This trail will give kids a close-up view of massive fins and monoliths. In the springtime, study the subtle and not-so-subtle colors of the wildflowers at your feet while listening to the quiet of the desert around you.

Some longer hikes can be enjoyed in **Devils Garden,** across from the entrance to the campground. The trail passes several arches and offers views of the **Fins, Salt Wash** and the **LaSal Mountains.** The total loop from the trailhead to **Double O Arch** and back along the primitive trail through **Fin Canyon** is five miles. A self-guiding trail booklet, available at the Visitor Center and at the trailhead, provides information on the trail features. Elevational gain from the trailhead to **Double O Arch** is 200 feet. The first mile to **Landscape Arch,** a thin formation that is the longest in the park, is easy and can be enjoyed by most families. The **Devils Garden Trail** is one my family comes back to time and time again, largely because there are a number of side trails and many options. Even the five-mile round-trip trail isn't beyond the capabilities of many children, though it can be a hot and dry trek in the middle of the summer.

The most famous hike in Arches is the one-mile (one way) trek to **Delicate Arch.** After viewing historic **Wolfe Ranch,** this trail (with its

Delicate Arch

480-foot elevation gain), will be a challenge, especially during the hot summer. When hiking in July and August, try this one at sunrise or sunset. Kids will delight in walking across the swinging foot-bridge over **Salt Wash**. Then, take them across polished red slickrock from rock cairn to rock cairn. The trail is designed so that the **Delicate Arch** isn't seen until the last minute. When you finally see this arch, it will take your breath away. A word of caution is in order, though. This hike involves a steady climb and isn't recommended for very young children, unless you plan on carrying them part of the way.

Kids also love campfire programs. And the ones at the campfire circle near the Arches campground are unique because the program area is framed by the graceful **Skyline Arch**.

Arches remains one of the most accessible national parks in the United States. It is an excellent place to introduce your children to the joys of Utah's National Parks.

Bryce Canyon

Bryce Canyon National Park is a place where children can put their imaginations to good use. As they walk through a maze of soft, brilliant red, orange and beige limestone, where every turn of a corner produces an oddly-shaped fin, window, arch or crevice, they can't help but be amazed by this wonderland of eroded rock.

Campgrounds at Bryce Canyon are in an alpine setting. Because of high elevations, camping here is a bit cooler than many of Utah's national parks. At least one camping area is open year-round, but expect to pitch your tent or set up your camper in the snow during the winter. Lodging is available within the park from May through September at the recently-remodeled **Bryce Canyon Lodge**, which also has a dining room and gift shop. Lodging just outside of the park is available year-round.

The easiest way to see Bryce Canyon with children is to spend a day enjoying the views of the canyon from the various parking areas and viewpoints. Looking down on the **Bryce Amphitheater** (Bryce isn't really a canyon at all!) from places like **Bryce Point, Inspiration Point** and **Sunset Point** will give both children and adults a feel for this park. So will hiking along the rim trail, an alternative that will surely be suggested by the naturalist at the visitor center as soon as a parent asks about activities available for children.

You may be tempted to explore Bryce Canyon further by actually walking down into the unbelievably beautiful crimson-colored cliffs and rock formations this park is famous for. Children, if they are over five or six years of age, will see other children hike in what looks like a fairyland of brightly colored rock formations and hidden trails, and will beg for a

Queen's Garden Trail at Bryce

chance to do some exploring on their own. This will force parents into making a difficult decision. Are you willing to take the easy hike down into this wonderland, knowing that you will have to eventually make the steep climb back out?

There are ways to avoid enduring that return climb out of Bryce Canyon on foot, however. If your children are over five years of age and the family vacation budget allows it, the most obvious way is to take a two-hour or one-half day horseback riding trip into and out of the canyon. This will cost anywhere from $12 to $20 per person. These rides are offered from about mid-April through mid-October.

A hike that we've enjoyed with our youngest son, Bryer, who was four at the time, involved shuttling cars. This is easy when traveling with another family. If not, either Mom or Dad will be forced to miss this trek of about four miles. Start the hike at either **Sunset Point** or **Sunrise Point** on the top of the **Bryce Amphitheater** and walk toward the town of Tropic. Ask the ranger at the visitor center where to leave your car at the bottom. The walk downhill is easy and you can drive back to the top of Bryce Canyon when it is over.

If that is too complicated or the four miles a bit long, the least strenuous hike below the rim is the 1.5-mile **Queen's Garden Trail**, which takes about two hours to complete and climbs 320 feet. Other hikes feature elevation drops of 750, 521 and 827 feet. They can be done with children, but expect to do some cajoling and carrying of children on hot summer days. The rewards for taking the time to try one of these hikes are great. The trails lead through a maze of rock formations colored by the iron oxides and manganese found in the sediments. To a child, this will seem like a fairyland.

For a more solitary experience at Bryce, try taking a hike through one of the meadows you will see away from the crowded amphitheater. In the

Great Horned Owl

spring, sego lilies, penstemons, asters, clematis, evening primrose, scarlet gilias, Indian paintbrush and wild iris turn the park into a wildflower garden. My daughter likes to dance through a meadow at twilight, becoming a queen with a thousand subjects. But, please tell your children not to pick the flowers. Leave them for the next family to enjoy.

Bryce Canyon offers many interpretive programs throughout the summer. During most years, kids' naturalist programs will be held at least three times a week. Possible topics include "Tracking the Animals," "Exploring the Forest" and "Things You'll Find in the Forest." Check with the visitor center for times and dates.

Bryce's weather is among the most diverse in southern Utah. Pleasant days and cool nights prevail April through October with thunderstorms common during the summer. Winter lasts from November to March and is one of the best times to visit Bryce Canyon. We took a memorable snowshoeing trip into Queen's Garden with our children when the twins were five and my daughter was six. We happened to hit Bryce Canyon on a clear, beautiful winter day and had the park to ourselves. Seeing the white snow on red rock was a thrill and, though the climb out of the canyon was steadily uphill, the children enjoyed the novelty of hiking with snowshoes. They are provided free by the National Park Service at the Visitor Center. Cross country skiing along the rim trail is also enjoyable. Fall and spring are a great time to visit Bryce Canyon, though hiking can be difficult following a rainstorm because the trails get muddy.

Canyonlands

This southeastern Utah park is a place where children can play hide and seek in hidden sandstone alcoves or hike to ancient Indian ruins. It is a park where they can ride their BMX bicycles over exciting dirt roads or experience the thrill of walking through a passage two feet wide with sandstone cliffs several hundred feet high on either side of them.

Developed facilities are limited at Canyonlands, which is divided into three distinct districts. There is no in-park lodging and it is best to bring everything you need with you when visiting. The only developed campground with drinking water is the **Squaw Flat** Campground in the **Needles District**. Don't let lack of developed facilities discourage you from visiting Canyonlands.

Needles District

With its camping sites spread far away from one another and guarded by interesting rock formations of all shapes, sizes and hues, children will be delighted simply camping at **Squaw Flat**. Large amounts of time can be

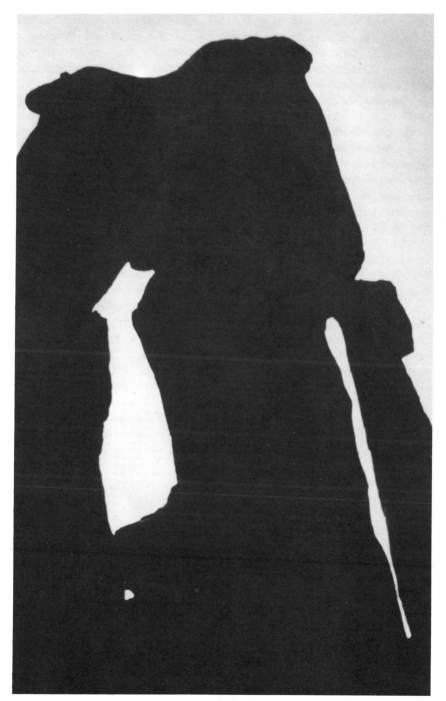

Druid Arch

spent sitting in camp and letting the kids explore nearby alcoves where their imaginations will wisk them away into a world of enchantment. Before you let them go, however, check out the area and set strict rules of behavior. There are a few dangerous cliffs near the campgrounds where children might get into trouble.

Perhaps the most accessible hiking areas in Canyonlands are found in the Needles District, reached by turning west on Highway 191 between Moab and Monticello to Highway 211 and then driving 34 miles to **Squaw Flat Campground**. One paved road ends just past the campground at **Elephant Hill**, one of the most challenging jeep trails in the United States. There are three short nature hikes in this area and, on the first day's visit, there may be time to examine all three. The interpretive pamphlets at the trailhead will quickly introduce families to the Indian lore, cowboy history and slickrock geology of Canyonlands. If your kids are like mine, these short hikes will stimulate their imagination so much they'll beg you to stay longer at Canyonlands.

You might want to try the self-guided trail to **Roadside Ruin** first. The trail begins just past the Needles Ranger District office and leads to a small ancient Indian ruin. In addition to telling about the ancient Indians who once inhabited Canyonlands, this trail will introduce children to the desert plants and ecology, including an unusual plant community called cryptogamic soil. This crusty-looking soil may look like ordinary dirt, but is actually composed of several species of mosses, fungi and algae. Try not to destroy or walk on this soil. It protects the desert from erosion, absorbs moisture and provides nitrogen and other nutrients for plant growth.

The other two nature trails in the Needles District are also short and easy. **Cave Spring** is located near the rangers' residences. This trail takes

Longnose Leopard Lizard

hikers across level ground where children get a chance to walk under a massive alcove. Let them crawl into its far corner to discover just how big it is. The trail then climbs up slickrock for approximately two-tenths of a mile. Kids will be thrilled to discover that they must climb down two old, wooden ladders leading to Cave Spring and an old cowboy line camp located in a deep alcove. My kids talked about this trail for days. A detailed brochure, which can be picked up at the trailhead for Cave Spring, tells about the history of the cowboy camp.

The third nature trail in the Needles area is called **Pothole Point**. It can be found by driving toward **Big Spring Canyon Overlook**. This little trail introduces Cedar Mesa Sandstone and the small depressions in it called "potholes." These potholes are often dry in the summer but, when they are filled with water by cloudbursts, special pothole dwellers like snails, fairy shrimp, clam shrimp, tadpole shrimp and horsehair worms will quickly breed and lay eggs.

After hiking these trails, parents will be forced to make a decision. They can either continue their vacation elsewhere or choose a longer but slightly more difficult Needles District hike. Another choice they might make would be to travel back to Moab or Monticello and sign up for a guided jeep trip or river running expedition to further explore these canyons, rivers and dirt roads. My experience with kids in jeeps, however, is that after a short while, they often get tired and bored and will want to get out and do something else. The best tours combine jeeping with many stops for short hikes. Mountain bikes also can be rented in Moab and are a quiet way to explore Canyonlands' many jeep trails. They are not allowed on the hiking trails, however, and you will have to watch children closely on some of the steeper overlooks. My twins took their BMX bicycles to Canyonlands and enjoyed riding them on some of the dirt roads. They did, however, require close supervision.

There are a number of all-day hikes in the Needles District. A good one to try if you have children five years of age or older is the six-mile (round trip) trail to **Chesler Park**. There is a steep climb at the start of the trail— near **Elephant Hill**—but the rest is fairly flat and easy. A word of caution is in order, however, This hike can be extremely hot in the summer, so take plenty of water. The walk winds its way through sandstone slickrock and narrow passages. Hikers can see scenic views of the sandstone fins that give the Needles Disetrict its name as they walk across the tops of ridges. For those able to walk just a little further, the eight-tenths of a mile **Joint Trail** is well worth the extra effort. Beginning on the west side of the **Needles** in **Chesler Canyon**, this trail proceeds through a narrow passage caused by subterranean forces shifting and fracturing the overlying rocks. There are several longer and slightly more difficult hikes in the Needles District, as well as some rugged jeep trails.

Island in the Sky District

The Island in the Sky District of Canyonlands is reached by taking Dead Horse Point State Park road off Utah 1919 and driving east. It is easier to see than it has been in the past because the National Park Service is in the process of paving it. There are two interpretive trails with brochures in this area. These include the **Mesa Arch** and **Upheaval Dome** trails.

The **Mesa Arch Trail** is a one-half-mile loop and winds its way through the pinyon-juniper woodland to the edge of the plateau. Here a hiker can view the high LaSal Mountains and a second arch framed by the **Mesa Arch** at the trail's most distant point.

The short (30-minute) hike at **Upheaval Dome**, located near **Upheaval Dome Picnic Area**, will explain Canyonlands' geology. There are some sheer cliffs at the overlook, so watch your children closely.

The **Whale Rock Trail** is another easy hike (although it has a 100 foot elevation gain) found in the Island in the Sky District. **Whale Rock** forms part of the outer **Upheaval Dome**. From the top of Whale Rock, a hiker views **Trail Canyon** to the east and the western portion of **Island in the Sky Mesa**.

There are a number of other day hikes in Island of the Sky District. Take water with you. Even in the small primitive campground in this area, there is no water. The closest water is at nearby Dead Horse Point State Park.

Grandview Point at Canyonlands

Grandview Point at Canyonlands

Pictographs at Horseshoe Canyon

Maze District

The most difficult area of Canyonlands to see is the Maze District. To get here, you will need to take a 60-mile ride over a dirt road. There are some unusual things to see here. In fact, the places which are most difficult to reach often have the most to offer. Only about 6,000 folks a year make the effort to get to the Maze.

Horseshoe Canyon's famous Indian rock art is the easiest attraction to reach in this section. The pictographs are found at the end of a trail on a separate unit of Canyonlands in its far northwestern corner. They were left by Indians perhaps as many as 3,000 years ago and feature haunting lifesize forms in what is known as the **Great Gallery**.

Another fine hike for older children is deep into the **Maze** itself, where they can view the famous **Harvest Scene** pictographs. The aptly-named **Chocolate Drops** can be seen from the primitive campground at the overlook. The hike into the Maze involves crawling and scrambling six-tenths of a mile with a vertical drop of 600 feet down a slickrock trail. Parts are so steep hikers must use footholds and handholds carved into the sandstone. Hiking the Maze, a box-like canyon complex, is an adventure in map reading. It is easy to get lost here, so take a topographical map and know how to read it before venturing into the canyons. A few freshwater springs are found at the bottom of the Maze. Purify this water before drinking it.

There are four primitive campgrounds in the Maze District, none with water. Three of them are on the **Flint Trail** road which leads to the **Land of the Standing Rocks**, the **Fins**, the **Wall**, **Lizard Rock** and **Chimney Rock**. This road dead ends at The Doll House, from where a trail goes down to the Colorado River and Cataract Canyon's Spanish Bottom.

Guided jeep and river running tours of Canyonlands National Park are available in Green River, Moab and Monticello. The ride through Cataract Canyon (plan on spending four or five days) on the Colorado River is more thrilling than any roller coaster kids will ever ride, but it is not recommended for children under six or for those who are afraid of water or do not swim well. Shorter, easier and less expensive trips on other parts of the Colorado and Green Rivers are available.

The weather at Canyonlands lends itself to year-round trips. It gets very hot in the summer. Temperatures can drop below freezing—with snow possible—in the winter. The mildest weather is usually found in the spring and fall.

Slickrock Fun

Capitol Reef

Capitol Reef National Park is a desert paradise for children. It combines history and hiking in an atmosphere where learning is easy. Many easy hikes can be enjoyed by even the youngest of children and interpretive programs will challenge kids to think about what they are seeing.

The campground at Capitol Reef, open year-round, is small and fills fast. There are no in-park lodging facilities, but there are motels in nearby Torrey, Hanksville and Bicknell. The weather is hot in the summer, can get cold in the winter and is mildest in the fall and spring.

There are eleven maintained hiking trails located near park headquarters. None are too difficult for kids over the age of six and most are easy to reach. Other hikes in more remote portions of the park — like the **Muley Twist Canyons** or the **Waterpocket Fold** — are more difficult and accessible only by dirt road. Check with the rangers for local conditions.

One of the finest children's hikes in Utah is the **Hickman Bridge** trail in Capitol Reef National Park. Its trailhead is located just off Utah Highway 24 in the center of the park. The hike's one-mile (one-way) length makes it a bit longer than most recommended treks for young children. There are potholes to explore, alcoves to hide in and unusual rock formations to discover. It is the only self-guided nature trail in Capitol Reef, though several others are in the planning stages. The informative booklet at the trailhead of the Visitor Center will answer many children's questions about the plant life and geology of Capitol Reef. The motivation for getting kids to finish the hike is a chance to see the **Hickman Bridge** at the end of the trail. It has been carved by water from the Kayenta sandstone into a massive formation. Plan on spending several hours walking this trail with youngsters. It might even be fun to pack a lunch. The trail takes time if you stop and let your children experience all the possibilities in this desert playground.

There are many other easy hikes in Capitol Reef. In fact, some of them — mostly notably the **Grand Wash** and **Capitol Gorge** trails — can be attempted by even the youngest of children. Don't be afraid to let kids stop and explore an alcove, play in the sand or study some pebbles. Let yourself see these trails through their eyes. You can learn much from them. My kids especially enjoyed **Capitol Gorge Trail** because there were a number of little holes eroded in the steep Navajo sandstone walls they could crawl into and hide. There are also children's hikes along the **Fremont River**, at **Cohab Canyon** and to **Chimney Rock**. None of these are overly difficult, and each offers unique and varied opportunities to teach children about the desert environment. **Grand Wash**, for example, is a level two-mile hike along a wash bottom framed by perpendicular sandstone walls. The one-mile **Fremont River** hike is easy for the first one-half mile and then becomes more strenuous. It begins with a level walk through the orchards near the

Fruita Schoolhouse at Capitol Reef

Hiking at Capitol Reef

river and then climbs to the overlook of the canyon and the valley. **Cohab Canyon** is difficult for the first one-fourth mile and then moderate for the next mile as it climbs to a hidden canyon high above the campground. Short side trails lead to overlooks. **Chimney Rock** is a three-mile loop trail requiring a slightly strenuous climb up switchbacks and a moderate hike on the upper loop with views of Chimney Rock from below and above with panoramas of surrounding areas.

One of the most enjoyable things about a trip to Capitol Reef with the kids is that there are a few alternatives to hiking that will add to their vacation experience.

One such activity involves a visit to the old **Fruita schoolhouse**, which is staffed in the summer on Thursday, Friday and Saturday by volunteers from the Daughters of the Utah Pioneers. Some of these volunteers were once students at the school. They tell visitors stories about their memories of those times. There is also a recorded message, in which one of the former teachers reminisces about her experiences there. A handout detailing the historic uses of the school is provided upon request at the visitor center. An old blacksmith and farm equipment shop, located near the group camping area, interprets local history in much the same way. Again, a recorded message helps children visualize what farm life must have been like in this area in the pioneer days.

Families re-create history when fruit trees in the old Capitol Reef orchards are ready to yield ripe fruit. Fruit may be picked without restrictions when ripe in a few "unposted" orchards. These are orchards in the campground, picnic area and around the schoolhouse. In "posted" orchards visitors can enjoy all the fruit they can eat. Fruit may be carried out of posted orchards, however, only when the park has designated an orchard as being "open" for picking. A park employee is usually on duty in these orchards and a nominal fee per pound is charged. When picking fruit, children should be accompanied by a responsible adult. The main fruit crops at Capitol Reef are cherries, apricots, peaches, pears and apples. The harvest usually begins in late June or early July and runs through mid-October.

The fruit trees and the old schoolhouse are part of Capitol Reef's rich history. In 1880, Nels Johnson built the first permanent cabin in Capitol Reef and planted crops. New families began to arrive and, after much hard work, the developing community became a resupply point for travelers on the rugged Capitol Gorge trail. A barn, farmhouse, rock fence and the 1896 schoolhouse still stand and allow visitors to the park a look into the past. The town the Mormon settlers built here came to be known as Fruita because of the many fruit trees they planted.

Canyon Overlook Trail at Zion

Zion

It was an ordinary late summer afternoon when I first visited Zion National Park. I was on a business trip and, never having seen a national park in Utah, I took a slightly longer route so I could drive through Zion Canyon.

To say that its massive canyon walls were impressive would be an understatement. As formations like the Great White Throne, the West Temple and the Towers of the Virgin loomed over the Virgin River like oversized red rock fortresses, the beauty of Zion National Park overwhelmed me. My only regret was not stopping to see more.

Starting with a trip on my honeymoon and continuing with many family vacations since then, I've returned to Zion time and time again. With each visit, I have seen more. There was the breath-taking beauty of the waterfalls on a hike to the Emerald Pools in a driving rain storm, the dizzying, hot June hike to Angels Landing and the quiet fall trip where the colors of the leaves in the canyon bottoms matched the canyon walls in splendor.

From May to October, the temperatures at Zion range from 72 to 105 degrees during the day and from 45 to 73 in the evening. Thus, Zion can be visited anytime with the most crowded conditions occurring in the summer. Campgrounds are large and space is usually available. There is lodging within the park from April to November at the Zion Lodge, which also has a snack bar, restaurant and gift shop. Lodging and private campgrounds with showers and utility hookups are available just outside the park in Springdale or Mt. Carmel.

As a father, I've found Zion National Park is a place I return to again and again with my children. There are some activities for kids here that won't be found elsewhere.

For example, there is the **Junior Ranger Program** at the **Zion Nature Center**. Here children ages six through twelve can learn about the park five days a week, from June to early August. The Nature Center was established in 1974 and averages 1,000 participants during the summer weeks when it is offered. The program is sponsored by Zion National Park and the Zion Natural History Association with a nominal one-time registration fee to defray the cost of the Junior Ranger awards.

The program is designed to provide a learning experience for children seeking knowledge about Zion. Those attending classes can expect to learn about wildlife protection, local history and conservation while enjoying the beauty and wonder of nature. The center itself is located just north and within walking distance of the South Campground. Registration is in the morning and afternoon of each class day. The program runs Tuesday through Saturday with different activities each day. Children may attend one or more classes.

Another interesting annual event held at Zion National Park is the Southern Utah Folklife Festival. This event happens on the Thursday, Friday and Saturday after Labor Day. Pioneer crafts, history, poetry, storytelling, the making of pioneer food, children's folklife, Indian folkways and demonstrations and displays make this an enjoyable family experience.

Another way to introduce children to Zion National Park is to pre-order a kids' book from the Zion Natural History Association, Zion National Park, Springdale, Utah 84767. Ask for the Zion Adventure Guide, which costs $1.95 and has a number of excellent activities your children will enjoy on the car ride on the way to the park.

While some of the hikes at Zion National Park are long and strenuous, there are several which are appropriate for children.

My favorite is the 1.2-mile round trip hike to the **Lower Emerald Pool**. This hike, on a paved trail, can be reached by parking across from the **Zion Lodge**. The lower pool is formed by a waterfall that arches over the trail. The look on a child's face, when he or she discovers the trail leads behind this cascading water, can make an entire trip to Zion worthwhile. We took this hike during a spring rainstorm, and it seemed as though waterfalls were everywhere. The flowing water creates a sense of adventure and accents the beautiful green foliage of the red-walled canyons. If your kids are as enthusiastic about walking on the **Emerald Pools Trail** as mine were, they'll also want to hike to the **Upper Pool**, which is larger and sits at the base of a high

Chief Interpreter Victor Jackson at Zion Nature Center

cliff. Be careful here. Kids will want to look over the sandstone edge at the **Middle Pool**. The dropoff is steep and the rock can be slippery. Still, the extra walk completes a loop trail and is worth the effort. Guided ranger walks are available to Emerald Pools from March through October.

For people who enjoy interpretive walks, there are three self-guided nature trails in Zion.

Weeping Rock is a one-half-mile trail taking an hour to complete. The trail ends at Weeping Rock, a rock alcove with dripping springs. Hanging gardens of wildflowers decorate the walls in spring and summer.

The **Canyon Overlook Trail**, about one-half mile in length, takes about an hour to complete. It features a self-guided trail book. It ends with a spectacular viewpoint of lower **Zion Canyon, Pine Creek Canyon** and the **Zion-Mt. Carmel Highway** switchbacks. This trail will give visitors a feeling

Canyon Overlook Trail at Zion

Emerald Pool Waterfall at Zion

for this canyon country. After that, try taking a two-hour, one-mile trek up the **Gateway to the Narrows**, which follows the **Virgin River** upstream to the **Zion Canyon Narrows** where the paved trail ends. Hanging gardens of wildflowers in the spring and summer enhance what is already a beautiful walk. The most impressive thing about this hike, however, are the perpendicular sandstone cliffs which tower above you on either side.

Another more strenuous hike often suggested by park naturalists, especially in the spring, fall and winter months, is the **Watchman Trail**. It begins at the **South Campground Amphitheater** and ends at a viewpoint of **Lower Zion Canyon, Oak Creek Canyon** and the town of **Springdale**.

There are other longer hikes at Zion for older children. The trek to **Angels Landing**, for example, is a memorable one for kids over ten who can be trusted to follow instructions. The hike involves holding onto some chains near a steep overlook and is not for the faint of heart.

Horseback riding is available in Zion National Park from commercial outfitters for fees ranging from $8.25 to $45.00 per person, depending on the length of the ride. Compared to many areas, their rates are relatively inexpensive. Kids must be five or older to ride. The one-hour ride might be enough to give children their first taste of what a horseback ride is all about.

Kids love guided hikes and other ranger activities. Zion offers more of this type of activity than any other park in Utah. All of the scheduled interpretive programs run daily from April to October and are open to children. These include the traditional guided walks, illustrated evening programs and the popular **Naturalist Choice** demonstrations. People interested in these activities should check bulletin boards throughout the park or ask to see a current schedule at the visitor centers.

Sego Lily / Utah State Flower

Emerald Pool Trail at Zion

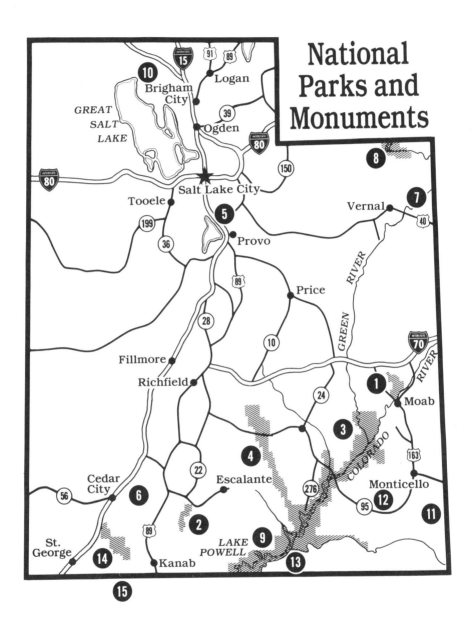

National Parks and Monuments

1 ARCHES
   NATIONAL PARK

2 BRYCE CANYON
   NATIONAL PARK

3 CANYONLANDS
   NATIONAL PARK

4 CAPITOL REEF
   NATIONAL PARK

5 TIMPANOGOS CAVE
   NATIONAL MONUMENT

6 CEDAR BREAKS
   NATIONAL MONUMENT

7 DINOSAUR
NATIONAL MONUMENT

8 FLAMING GORGE NATIONAL
RECREATION AREA

9 GLEN CANYON NATIONAL
RECREATION AREA

10 GOLDEN SPIKE NATIONAL
HISTORIC SITE

11 HOVENWEEP
NATIONAL MONUMENT

12 NATURAL BRIDGES
NATIONAL MONUMENT

13 RAINBOW BRIDGE
NATIONAL MONUMENT

14 ZION
NATIONAL PARK

15 PIPE SPRING
NATIONAL MONUMENT

Squirrel

Dinosaur National Monument

CHAPTER TWO

National Monuments

Think back to your childhood. When you played games in the back yard there was time to dream. Some days it was cowboys and Indians. On other occasions, trains were formed with tricycles and play cars. Or you imagined you were exploring a secret cave in your basement. On days when imaginations really ran wild, the back yard would turn into a primeval world inhabited by dinosaurs and wild beasts.

Indians. Trains. Caves. And dinosaurs — Topics that fascinate any child. For many children in America, these subjects can only be viewed on television or explored in books. For kids fortunate enough to travel in Utah, the subjects of these dreams can be touched.

Four of Utah's six national monuments — **Hovenweep**, **Golden Spike**, **Timpanogos Cave** and **Dinosaur** — deal directly with Indians, trains, caves and dinosaurs. The other two, **Cedar Breaks** and **Natural Bridges**, have their own appeal. Another, **Pipe Spring National Monument**, located on the Arizona side of the Utah-Arizona border, is included because it is part of Utah's heritage.

The national monuments are not as well known as the state's five national parks, but they are every bit as interesting.

Before traveling to the monuments, it is wise to write for information. Attractions at **Cedar Breaks** and **Timpanogos Cave**, for example, are closed in the winter. Hours at **Golden Spike** vary greatly, and the best interpretive activities at **Dinosaur** are usually found during the summer.

Here are some ideas on what these six areas can offer you and your family in the way of recreational and educational experiences:

Dinosaur

Before taking a trip to Dinosaur National Monument, on the Utah-Colorado border 19 miles east of Vernal, spark your kids' interest in dinosaurs. That shouldn't be difficult, since kids are naturally fascinated by prehistoric creatures. Libraries are full of children's books about dinosaurs. Trips to the Museum of Natural History on the University of Utah campus, the Utah Field House of Natural History in Vernal, the Cleveland-Lloyd Dinosaur Quarry in Emery County or the College of Eastern Utah Prehistoric Museum in Price will enhance further a child's curiosity.''

After all of the preparation, one of your children may ask a simple question that won't be easy to answer.

"But, Daddy," a child may ask as he looks at a fully assembled skeleton of a dinosaur, "where do all those bones come from?"

When you hear that question, it's time to take your trip to Dinosaur National Monument. Its big attraction is the **Dinosaur Quarry**, located seven miles north of U.S. 40 and the town of **Jensen**. The main quarry is inside a building where National Park Service paleontologists continue to uncover fossil bones, leaving them in place in the rock. A shuttle bus is operated during the busy summer season to get visitors from their cars to the quarry. Rangers are on hand to explain that these fossilized bones are not found together in one piece like those seen at museums. Rangers will also explain how the bones got here, why they are so jumbled (they were collected and buried by a river) and how paleontologists study the bones to learn more about dinosaurs and their environment.

Dinosaur Quarry at Dinosaur National Monument

Western
Rattlesnake

the geology of areas where dinosaur bones are found.

The National Park Service (funds permitting) sponsors a junior paleontologist program each day at the quarry for youngsters who have completed second, third or fourth grade during the past year. These 45-minute programs explore the world of fossils. If your kids want to participate in this program, sign them up early. Spots are limited.

There are other things to see at this monument, which encloses more than 320 square miles of scenic canyon country. There are short nature trails at **Split Mountain, Lodore** and along the **Harpers Corner Scenic Drive**, as well as a few longer trails at **Jones Hole** and other areas. During the summer, rangers offer a variety of activities at the **Dinosaur Quarry** and other sites.

Split Mountain Campground, near the Dinosaur Quarry, has 35 campsites and is open year-round. An additional 100 summer-only sites are at the nearby Green River Campground. Both have modern restrooms and drinking water. There are five other more primitive camping areas on both the Utah and Colorado sides of the monument.

Commercial concessionaires offer guided one to five-day raft trips from late spring through early fall on the **Green** and **Yampa Rivers**. The one-day trips are good introductions to rafting for children and reasonably priced. For information, write to the Superintendent, Dinosaur National Monument, Box 210, Dinosaur, Colorado 81610.

Dinosaur National Monument Shuttle

A Dinosaur Puzzle at Dinosaur National Monument

Timpanogos Cave

Timpanogos Cave National Monument, located in American Fork Canyon southeast of Salt Lake City, has been a traditional destination for family outings. Many Utahns who do very little hiking otherwise make the strenuous 1.5-mile trek — with its 1,065-foot elevation gain — an "annual" event. This paved self-guided nature trail is not an easy walk, but people of all ages can and do enjoy it each year.

The cave system itself consists of three small limestone caves full of different types of limestone formations. Guided tours through the interconnected caverns are conducted by National Park Service rangers. Since the average cave temperature is 43 degrees, you may want to carry a light jacket or sweater up the trail with you.

Nominal tour prices are charged, with discounts for children and senior citizens. The operating season is largely determined by when the snow flies, but the caves are usually open from mid-May through October. On Saturdays and holidays more visitors want tours than the cave will hold.

Trail to Timpanogos Cave

Timpanogos Cave National Monument

Available tickets are often sold by afternoon.

The best time to take your family on this hike and cave tour is during the week. The National Park Service, realizing many Utah residents have seen the caves many times, has added interesting variations to the cave tours. Families may find these more interesting than the regular tour. The unusual tours include candlelight excursions, flashlight tours, photography exhibitions and historic lectures. Some of these special tours can turn a visit to the cave into an adventure of the imagination. Check with the monument for times and dates of these special tours. In addition, rangers offer guided nature walks and geology hikes.

When hiking to the cave with your kids, expect them to get tired. We bring water and "bribes" (in the form of trail mix or candy) to keep ours going. We encourage them to find the next numbered post on the guided nature trail and to search for familiar animals and plants. If your youngsters are under six, plan on carrying them part of the way. Benches are provided for rest along the way because this isn't an easy hike. When you reach the cave, your children will be proud of themselves; because they have completed a difficult hike to earn their tour of the cave. A word of caution is in order, however. The lights are almost always turned out in the cave at one point during the tour, to let visitors experience the total darkness of a cave. If your kids are afraid of the dark, you would do well to prepare them for this.

There are no camping facilities at Timpanogos Cave National Monument, but there are nearby U.S. Forest Service campgrounds in the Uinta National Forest.

Hovenweep

This small national monument, tucked away in the extreme corner of southeastern Utah, is not well known. It is located 16 miles east of the **Hatch Trading Post** on a dirt road system and is near the four corners of Utah, Colorado, New Mexico and Arizona. In fact, if you visit Hovenweep with your children, you should take the short drive to the place where they can stand in all four states at once. This is the only place in the entire United States where that can be done.

All approach roads to Hovenweep are graded dirt roads that can become muddy during or following a storm. If the weather is wet, make local inquiry about road conditions. There is a modern campground near the ranger station, but food, gas and supplies must be brought from home. There are no stores within several miles of Hovenweep.

Hovenweep is a monument that can be seen in a few hours. We have included it in Indian ruin theme vacations in the **Four Corners** area along with places like Colorado's Mesa Verde National Park, New Mexico's

Ruin at Hovenweep National Monument

Chaco Canyon National Monument and Arizona's Canyon de Chelly National Monument. All are within a day's drive of one another. Children are usually interested in the Indian ruins found in these historical areas.

Kids should have no trouble hiking the three short loop trails in Hovenweep that take about 90 minutes. These trails lead to the **Square Tower Ruin Group**. A self-guided trail booklet available from the ranger station will help you understand the things you are seeing while on the trail. This is an easy trail to hike, with close-up views of the ruins, and is a good place to begin a journey into the land where the Anasazi Indians once lived. The Square Tower Ruins, the best preserved and most impressive in the area, are noted for their square, oval, circular and D-shaped towers.

Another hiking trail connects the Square Tower Ruin Group with three other groups of ruins. This trek is approximately eight miles long, so plan on walking most of the day. Carry water and ask for a small topographic map at the ranger station.

The National Park Service, largely because of budget constraints, offers few interpretive programs or activities designed for children in this small, remote monument. But, when school groups visit the area, rangers present programs on sketching, Anasazi foods, archaeological techniques, water control techniques, astronomy and the preservation of archaeological resources. Rangers hope to adopt some of these programs for the general public in the form of handouts that children can work on independently.

Natural Bridges

Ideally, all family vacations should be learning experiences. Your children should come away from Natural Bridges National Monument, located in an isolated part of southeastern Utah 42 miles west of Blanding, with two new bits of knowledge.

They will learn the difference between a natural bridge and an arch (which they can view at Arches National Park, located about three hours north of Natural Bridges. A natural bridge is formed by flowing water while an arch is formed by wind and rain.)

Three natural bridges are located within the boundaries of this national monument — **Owachomo, Sipapu** and **Kachina** — and are equally spectacular. While they can be viewed from roadside viewpoints (making it possible to see the entire monument in about an hour), I recommend a hike to all of the bridges. It is possible to hike to all three bridges with your children, but the easiest trek is the one-half mile round trip walk to **Owachomo Bridge**. On this trail, children can view the oldest bridge in the monument as well as note the forces of erosion that shaped it. Just on the other side of the bridge is **Armstrong Canyon**, an area where children might explore a streambed. Wildlife frequents this area, so have the kids keep quiet and watch closely.

There will be a temptation to make your visit to this monument a short one as you drive between Arches and Lake Powell. If you have the time,

Sipapu Bridge at Natural Bridges

Natural Bridges Hiking Trail

stop and enjoy Natural Bridges. The trails here have a great variety of desert scenery with potholes, washes and alcoves to explore. There are several easy all-day hikes that young children enjoy. Fall and spring are the best times to visit. The campground is primitive, with pit toilets, but campsites are spread out under a juniper forest. This is an excellent place for an overnight stay.

The second bit of knowledge your children should bring from Natural Bridges is that electricity can be generated by sunlight. The visitor center and ranger residences in the area receive 90 percent of their power from a solar photovoltaic system. Your kids will get a "charge" out of flipping a light switch that turns on a display operated by the nearby solar cells. This can open some interesting discussions about alternative energy sources.

Cedar Breaks

Cedar Breaks National Monument is a natural red rock amphitheater. It is more than 2,000 feet deep and three miles in diameter. Many visitors make a mistake by visiting the overlooks and then driving on. There are some short hikes leading through forests and out along the rim.

There is a small campground which fills up fast in the summer. Other national forest campgrounds are available nearby.

The monument is located 30 miles west of Panguitch and 22 miles north of Cedar City. It is near Bryce Canyon and Zion National Parks.

Kids are invited on all regularly scheduled walks. These are varied enough so they are interesting to adults and enjoyable to children. Interpretive walks are usually offered daily at 10:00 a.m. and 2:30 p.m. from late June through Labor Day, when the monument receives its heaviest visitation.

Trails include a two-mile self-guided trek to the **Alpine Pond**, and the two-mile long **Wasatch Ramparts Trail.** The Alpine Pond trail winds its way through high mountain meadows and is particularly pretty in late June and early July, when the snow has just melted and the wildflowers in the meadows are in bloom. The Wasatch Ramparts Trail passes a stand of ancient bristlecone pine at **Spectra Point** and ends at a viewpoint overlooking the **Cedar Breaks Amphitheater.** Neither trail is difficult, though you should watch your children closely as the trail winds near cliffs.

Kids should also find some activities of interest at the visitor center. Rangers say children enjoy testing rock samples for physical properties in a

Cougar

Cedar Breaks National Monument

geology exhibit. There is a touch table with samples of plant parts, bones and rocks which can be handled and examined. An animal track exhibit asks a child to guess what animal made a track and then compare his guess to an answer sheet. Upon request, park rangers will play a recording of mountain lion sounds which often fascinate children, especially those who will camp at Cedar Breaks.

Golden Spike

Golden Spike is a national historic site. It is located 32 miles west of Brigham City. To reach the site, drive west on Utah 83 to Promontory Junction, turn left, and follow the signs.

Kids are naturally drawn to trains. How many times have you driven down the highway when a train was rolling down the tracks nearby, only to have your kids start counting cars or looking for the caboose? A visit to Golden Spike National Historic Site will give your children a close-up view of some modern re-creations of the famous locomotives — Central Pacific's Jupiter and Union Pacific's 119 — which met on May 10, 1869 at this exact spot, thereby completing the route of the Transcontinental Railway. In the process, you will learn about the history of the railroad, the men who built it and the significance of the transcontinental railroad in the formation and modernization of the United States. Families should be impressed with the size of the locomotives.

Golden Spike National Monument

58

Golden Spike National Monument

The best time to visit Golden Spike is between May and September, when the replicas of the Jupiter and the 119 are operated daily. The primary visitor stop is at the **"Golden Spike Site."** To make the experience more realistic, a re-created site displays the vintage locomotives head-to-head on reconstructed tracks. Rangers conduct interpretive programs on a regular schedule.

There is an auto tour of the old Railroad Grade. Visitors can drive six miles of old railroad grade using a self-guided tour book. They can read about the work it took to lay ten miles of track in one day. A railroaders' festival in mid-August provides interpretive programs and displays as does the commemoration ceremony on May 10 at 11:30 a.m. each year. This features a re-enactment of the driving of the golden spike.

Facilities in the area are limited to a few picnic tables. There are no overnight lodging facilities or campgrounds within the historical site.

Pipe Spring

Though not in Utah, this small national historical area located on State Highway 59 (Arizona 389) between Hurricane and Kanab, Utah, has much to do with the Mormon history of the Beehive State. It also is located close to Lake Powell and Zion and Bryce Canyon National Parks.

Pipe Spring was discovered in 1858 by Mormon missionaries. Construction on the buildings preserved at the national monument started in 1870.

Living history exhibits celebrate this period of history. National Park Service interpreters dress in the costumes of the day to take visitors back in history. Some days, bread and cookies are cooked on a wood-burning stove. Local ranchers bring cattle to be branded on special days. Farms, blacksmith shops, ranch hands bunkhouses and the main ranch area — which resembles a fort — are preserved as they were during the late 1800s. A quiet nature trail with views of the vast Arizona Strip surrounds the monument.

This is a quiet stop which receives few visitors. It is a place my children have come to regard with great affection, largely because of the friendliness of the staff. Well off the beaten track, Pipe Spring is worth the effort needed to find it.

Mormon Tea

Bald Eagle

CHAPTER THREE

National Recreation Areas

The kids were paying close attention as I described in vivid detail what they would be doing on their newest adventure.

"Beware of 'Death Falls,'" I warned them as we loaded the raft onto the van. "We certainly don't want to hang the raft up on a rock like I did a few years ago. Why, that old rock just sucked me and all of my equipment right into the cold water. I was lucky to get out alive!"

I was, of course, joshing. The 7.3-mile stretch of the Green River between the Flaming Gorge Dam and the Little Hole Picnic Area is a good place to introduce your kids to rafting. But, as fathers know, there is nothing like building up a sense of adventure in the kids. If nothing else, it motivates them to obey when they are told they'll be required to wear a life jacket at all times.

The children looked up at the huge Flaming Gorge Dam as they prepared to board the raft. They felt the spray of the water in their faces and examined the steep canyon walls with mixed emotions. They were, of course, excited about this adventure. But what if all the things Dad was saying were true?

There were small stretches of "whitewater" that the kids viewed with trepidation, but nothing that Dad and Mom couldn't handle. We could see trout in the clear water. The excitement of paddling hard around the occasional rock kept the kids from becoming bored.

We were at the Flaming Gorge National Recreation Area in north-eastern Utah. It had been a relaxing vacation.

On the beach at Antelope Flat an antelope wandered through the campground while Dad was fishing for smallmouth bass. There was warm, shallow water where the kids could safely swim.

There were tours of the dam and Red Canyon Visitor Center, where the kids soon discovered why this place was named Flaming Gorge. Most of all, there was that night. Moments after a rainstorm had driven us under the covered picnic area, the sun's rays bathed the gorge to the west in orange

Pronghorn Antelope

and a magnificent double rainbow spanned the eastern horizon. As we smelled the freshly-caught bass sizzling on the old gas stove and felt the evening breeze, we savored every moment.

We've had times like that at the Glen Canyon National Recreation Area in southeastern Utah as well. There was the thrill of the twins each landing a six-pound striped bass nearly as big as they were, of telling stories around a crackling driftwood fire on a remote sandy beach, and swimming on a moonlit night when the water was smooth as glass.

Kids love water, and they'll find plenty of it at the Flaming Gorge and Glen Canyon National Recreation Areas. Both feature enormous man-made reservoirs surrounded by modern camping facilities. There are, however, some key differences to remember when planning a vacation to one of these waters.

Here is a look at what Utah's two national recreation areas have to offer:

Flaming Gorge

The Flaming Gorge National Recreation Area is managed by the U.S. Forest Service. Because of its relatively high elevation, it gets cold in the winter. The best time to visit is between May and September.

Many families take advantage of Flaming Gorge for boating and camping vacations. There are a number of small camping areas, as well as large campgrounds at **Firefighters Memorial, Lucerne Valley, Buckboard Crossing** and **Firehole**. Some of these are nestled in aspen and pine forests while others are in sagebrush flats.

One of the best "kid-oriented" places at Flaming Gorge is **Antelope Flat**, located north of Dutch John on Highway 260. The campground at Antelope Flat has been closed in recent years due to a lack of funds, but the boat launch and parking area remain open. A gradually sloping sandy beach and shallow water are the attractions here. Pronghorn antelope frequent the area, giving the kids the chance to see them at close range. The view of the Gorge is impressive from the covered picnic area. Expect a bit of a walk to the beach. Water levels fluctuate from year to year, making it a gravel beach at times and a weed-covered area at others. There are no lifeguards. We require our children to wear life jackets around the water.

Spring Creek, located beyond Antelope Flat on an undeveloped dirt road, has some shallow inlets for swimming. Another swimming beach is **Mustang Ridge's Sunny Cove**. There is a sandy beach next to this campground.

A must for a kids' trip to Flaming Gorge is a visit to the **Flaming Gorge Dam**. The visitor center, open from 9:30 a.m. to 5:00 p.m. from Memorial Day to Labor Day, is a good place to start. A movie — "Flaming Gorge: A Story Written in Water" — is presented every 90 minutes. Self-guided tours

Water Release from Flaming Gorge Dam

of the 502-foot high Flaming Gorge Dam are available daily from 8:00 a.m. to 4:00 p.m. between April and September. Children will enjoy looking down at the Green River far below them and then whisking down the elevator to the base of the dam where they learn how water flowing through large turbines creates electricity.

Water-oriented sports are the primary form of recreation at Flaming Gorge Reservoir. There are "boaters' campgrounds," accessible only by boat. Fishing at Flaming Gorge Reservoir is possible, but difficult. The reservoir is famous for its trophy lake and brown trout, but the angling generally isn't fast enough to hold a child's interest. Travel to nearby **Red Fleet Reservoir** or to places like **Browne, Spirit** or **Sheep Creek** lakes (a short drive away) to find better kids' fishing areas. Boat rentals are available at the **Cedar Springs Marina** near Dutch John, the **Lucerne Valley Marina** near Manila and the **Buckboard Marina** near Green River, Wyoming.

Taking a raft trip on the Green River below the Flaming Gorge Dam is a novel way to see the Recreation Area. Rafts can be rented for a reasonable fee at either **Dutch John Service** or **Flaming Gorge Lodge**. If you have two cars or enough adults to shuttle vehicles between the put-in point right below the Flaming Gorge Dam and **Little Hole**, 7.3 miles downstream, you'll save money because you won't have to hire someone to bring you and your raft back to Dutch John. It's possible to take two or three raft trips down this stretch of the river in a day, depending on how often you stop along the way. Kids will probably remember this portion of their vacation

Touring Flaming Gorge Dam

Red Canyon Overlook, Flaming Gorge National Recreation Area

more than any other. There are enough gentle rapids to keep the trip exciting. Make certain everyone is wearing a life jacket and try to stay out of the cold water. U.S. Forest Service officials recommend that rafters remember the "right rule." That is, when in doubt while floating the rapids on this river, keep right. The river can be dangerous, especially for the first-time rafters. Acquaint yourself with the rules and characteristics of the river before going in. Don't use a row boat or a cheap drugstore vinyl float. Don't overload rafts beyond the number of people recommended. Parents should emphasize caution when taking their children down this stretch of river. It is a fun river trip for amateurs, but caution is important.

Those who want to check out the Green River before taking a raft trip may want to hike the flat and gentle **Little Hole Trail** that follows the river. This trail is part of the National Recreation Trail system. Angling for nice-sized trout in the **Green River** is usually fast but be aware that no bait is allowed here and special regulations are in force. Because no bait can be used, younger children may have a difficult time fishing this stretch of river. This might be a chance for Dad or Mom to teach older kids the techniques of fly fishing or casting a spinner from shore. My twin sons soon tire of bait fishing, but love to cast a lure time after time. They've enjoyed this type of fishing since they were nine, a good age to introduce spincasting.

Families might also try to hike an easy trail network called the **Canyon Rim Trail** that extends from **Canyon Rim, Green's Lake** and the **Skull Creek Campgrounds** to the **Greendale Overlook**. These trails over rolling country are especially colorful in mid-May, when the wildflowers are in bloom. Nearby is **Red Canyon Visitor Center**, with a spectacular picture window view of Flaming Gorge Reservoir, 1,360 feet below the viewpoint. The center has exhibits depicting the area's plant and animal life, geology, cultural and human history and forest service management. Outside walkways provide additional views of the canyon. At times, you can see bighorn sheep from here. My kids spent one afternoon picking up litter all over the National Recreation Area and then turning it in at the Red Canyon Visitor Center. Their efforts were rewarded with a "prize packet" full of

Rainbow Trout / Utah State Fish

badges, coloring books and information. Before taking kids to Flaming Gorge, you might want to purchase a coloring and activity book called "Meet Flaming George" from the Flaming Gorge Natural History Association. This organization has a number of books available. For a publication list, write to Flaming Gorge Natural History Association, P.O. Box 188, Dutch John, Utah 84023.

The **Ute Mountain Lookout Tower** is the only such tower in Utah with living quarters remaining. It is on the National Register of Historic Places and is currently being restored by volunteers. It gives visitors a first-hand look at early forest fire detection. A recently-improved narrow road allows for access by vehicles with good clearance.

It may be reached from Highway 44 by turning west at the upper Sheep Creek junction onto the Hickerson Park Road (No. 222). Go about two miles and turn left onto road number 005. It's about a mile and a half down this road. The tower is open to the public from about mid-June to Labor Day.

Visiting Flaming Gorge is easy for families who don't wish to camp. The Flaming Gorge Lodge has modern motel units, a cafe and grocery store. Restaurants and grocery stores are found in nearby Manila and Dutch John.

For more detailed information on the area, write to the Ashley National Forest, Flaming Gorge Ranger District, P.O. Box 157, Dutch John, Utah 84023.

Red Canyon Visitor Center, Flaming Gorge

Ute Mountain Overlook

Houseboating at Lake Powell

Glen Canyon National Recreation Area

There isn't a bad time of year to take children on a visit to **Lake Powell**, part of the Glen Canyon National Recreation Area. The weather varies. Temperatures are in the 100s during the summer and below freezing at times during the winter. Lake Powell, under the management of the National Park Service, has its major recreation facilities at **Wahweap** near Page, Arizona, and at **Bullfrog Marina** west of Hanksville, Utah. Both areas have National Park-style campgrounds and areas with swimming beaches. No lifeguards are provided, so children in these areas need parental supervision. Smaller facilities are available at **Hite** and **Hall's Crossing** marinas.

The Del Webb Corporation manages private recreation on Lake Powell, including modern lodges at **Wahweap** and **Bullfrog** and marinas with boat rentals at **Bullfrog, Hite, Wahweap** and **Halls Crossing.**

Lake Powell is a boaters' paradise. Those who don't own a boat can rent one. Our family has rented a boat, packed all our camping gear into the bow, and headed out to find our own camping spot. We've found secluded beaches where the swimming was fabulous. We've caught catfish, striped and largemouth bass and crappie. We've used one of several commercially produced maps or guides to help us find our way to **Rainbow Bridge** or to explore arches and side canyons full of spectacular slickrock. Renting a 16- or 18-foot power boat is a relatively inexpensive way to see the reservoir.

The most relaxing way to see Lake Powell is to rent a houseboat. These boats sleep from six to twelve people and cost about the same per night as a

Glen Canyon National Recreation Area

good hotel. They have beds, baths, sinks, mirrors, toilets, showers and complete kitchens. Because they have "all the conveniences of home," houseboats allow families to explore Lake Powell's nearly 2,000 miles of shoreline in comfort. There are few vacations with children that will be quite as restful.

Once on Lake Powell — whether in a houseboat or a power boat — there are dozens of things to do. Find a remote canyon and let the kids hike, explore, or swim. There are dozens of hikes to places with alcoves, arches and Indian ruins on the lake.

The world's largest natural bridge is the feature of **Rainbow Bridge National Monument**. If you aren't the adventurous type and don't want to rent a boat to reach the bridge, guided tours on large crafts to Rainbow Bridge are available from both Bullfrog and Wahweap. Lunch is often provided.

The Del Webb Corporation sometimes organizes special programs geared for children 14 years of age and younger. For example, one summer it sponsored a bugle-mouth bass tournament. Bugle-mouth bass are, in reality, carp. The kid who caught the largest carp monthly was awarded a prize.

Information on tour prices, lodging and boat rentals at Lake Powell can be obtained by writing to Lake Powell, Del Webb Recreational Properties, Inc., 2916 North 35th Avenue, Suite 8, Phoenix, Arizona 85017-5261.

The National Park Service offers summer amphitheater programs at the **Wahweap** and **Bullfrog Campgrounds** during the summer vacation season. Rangers give talks on topics like wildlife and ancient Indians. The Park Service also presents a tour of the **Glen Canyon Dam** from June through September in conjunction with the Bureau of Reclamation. The **Carl Hayden Visitor Center** on the dam has displays and exhibits of interest to both adults and children. Check there for tour hours.

Hite Marina is a less developed facility on Lake Powell. There is highway access to the beaches here.

When visiting Lake Powell with your children, watch them closely around the water. Dropoffs can be very steep, and the reservoir is extremely deep in places. Kids twelve and under are required to wear life jackets while on any boat.

Weathered Juniper

Goblin Valley State Park

CHAPTER FOUR

State Parks

The sky had turned an ominous black over Goblin Valley State Park. Campers scurried to secure their tents and trailers in preparation for the downpour that would soon hit this remote recreation area.

Then, it began to rain. This wasn't an average rainstorm. Torrents came down from the sky, filling the desert with rushing water and erasing thousands of footsteps of previous visitors to this unusual natural preserve.

Perhaps it would have been wise to patiently sit in the car and wait for the storm to subside. That seemed most prudent under the circumstances.

But, as we sat and watched the storm develop, my wife decided it was time to see first-hand how our favorite state park was formed.

Goblin Valley has always seemed the epitome of a natural children's play area. Its small rock formations do indeed look like goblins. The little valley is a place with no established trails but dozens of the chocolate-drop shaped formations. Kids imagine themselves as knights in castles, cowboys and Indians or the conquerers of fortresses. The park is wonderful for playing hide and seek. At night, it is both eerie and mysterious especially when a full moon makes the goblins cast strange shadows.

Now, it was raining.

"Let's put on our rain ponchos and old boots," suggested my wife. "We've never seen it rain here before."

The kids, of course, were delighted at the prospect of this new adventure. There was none of the thunder and lightning that often accompanies such a desert storm, and the thought of playing in the rain seemed exciting.

Dad, ever the worrier, fought the notion at first. But, with hot showers in the nearby campground to clean up the mess that was certain to follow and more than a bit of curiosity himself, he consented to the hike.

The goblins are made of sandstone slightly harder than the surrounding layers. When dry, sand crumbles off when the goblins are touched.

In the rain, brown sand flowed from them in all directions. Signs of previous visitors to Goblin Valley were removed as little streams and trickles of dirty water appeared everywhere.

The small streams flowed to the lowest point in the valley, where a larger river suddenly materialized as if by magic. The river's water was the color of chocolate milk. (The children said it reminded them of the river in the movie "Willie Wonka and the Chocolate Factory.")

Though the river looked forboding, it was actually quite shallow and the kids took great delight in splashing through it. They tried to follow the snakelike meanders to see where they ended.

Just as suddenly as the desert storm started, it subsided. A bright orange light bathed the shining sandstone that forms Goblin Valley to create a surrealistic scene. Almost as quickly as they had started flowing, the streams and rivers were no more.

Ever the teacher, my wife took great pains to make certain the children were learning from this rare outdoor experience. She kept asking them to do more than play and to really look at what was happening around them.

"Why is it wet only two or three inches down before you get back to dry sand?" she asked. "Can you see how the water has carved the goblins into new shapes? Where do you think the water disappeared to when it stopped raining?" My wife knew the answers to some of these questions. Others would have to be answered later, either through research, more detailed thought, or by asking the ranger.

Yet, what could have been a boring two hours in the car became a memorable afternoon because we were open to encountering something new.

In a way, people unfamiliar with Utah often have to make that same jump when deciding to visit one of its 46 state parks.

Because of their accessibility and national reputation, Utah's national parks and monuments are relatively easy to find. Yet, because the state parks are off the beaten path, families traveling in Utah often bypass smaller treasures like Goblin Valley, Kodachrome Basin, Coral Pink Sand Dunes or Dead Horse Point State Parks.

Not all of Utah's state parks have the natural beauty of a Goblin Valley or Kodachrome Basin. In fact, many parks merely provide basic campground and beach facilities near major reservoirs. Others are museums and interpretive areas.

The state parks, however, offer some advantages not found at the national parks.

Most important, reservations can be made at any state park campground. Information on how to make reservations as well as a free brochure describing all the parks can be picked up at any state park or the Division of Parks and Recreation office at 1636 West North Temple, Suite 116, Salt Lake City, Utah 84116-3156.

Tyrannosaurus

Coral Pink Sand Dunes State Park

The address of each state park is listed in the appendix. Facilities at state park campgrounds vary from primitive to modern. A car entrance fee is charged at all the parks, though a season fun tag can be purchased by frequent park users. A special free fun tag for Utah senior citizens over 62 can be obtained for day use. Campground fees usually range from $5.00 to $10.00, depending on what the facilities offer.

The Utah State Parks system is still in its growing stage. New parks are being added while some areas remain relatively undeveloped. The system offers much in the way of family recreation, hosting thousands of visitors each year. Dozens of special activities are available as well, such as participating in living history events, motorcycle trips, sponsored bicycle tours and guided family equestrian rides.

Utah's state parks system can be divided into three major categories; heritage parks, natural areas, and water-oriented parks.

There are twelve major heritage parks which celebrate and explain the natural and cultural history of Utah by examining the archaeology, heritage, and flora and fauna of the state. Some are well developed. Others are relatively primitive.

There are natural areas — like Goblin Valley — that have been preserved for their scenic beauty. Many of these are in southern Utah and are hot in the summer. And, finally, there are many recreation and water-oriented state parks with basic camping and boat launching facilities near Utah's major reservoirs.

Here is an individual look at Utah's state parks and what they have to offer:

The Natural Areas

BONNEVILLE SALT FLATS — A world famous landmark, the Salt Flats are famed as the speedway where world land speed records are set. The state park here is undeveloped and consists of little more than an interpretive sign at the end of the pavement, five miles east of Wendover. Much of the Salt Flats themselves are owned and managed by the Bureau of Land Management.

On the surface, there appears to be nothing for a family to do at the Bonneville Salt Flats but look at miles of gleaming white salt with no sign of life. The biggest lure of this area is watching the race cars during speed week in late summer.

Yet, during times when the Great Salt Lake isn't too high and travel across the Salt Flats isn't dangerous, families might consider spending a night on the salt as ours did once during a meteor shower. Tell your kids to imagine that they are camping on the moon. The sky is amazingly clear here. The sun often rises like a huge orange ball over the sparkling salt crystals that make up the Salt Flats. In the fall the Salt Flats course is usually dry enough to drive a car on (check locally to see if it is safe) and the heat isn't oppressive. The experience isn't for everyone, but my family will never forget its night there.

CORAL PINK SAND DUNES — What could be more fun for children than a gigantic sand pile, full of nothing but fine pink sand?

This was the first place we took our twin sons on a camping trip. They were just over a year old at the time and delighted in crawling up and then rolling down the large dunes, building sand castles, burying themselves in the fine pink sand and drawing pictures with their fingers. The obligatory cleanup after a day on the ground consisted of merely a pat here and there and an emptying of shoes.

There are 22 camping units. The restrooms have showers with hot and cold running water.

Located 27 miles northwest of Kanab, the dunes are a convenient place to stop between Zion National Park, Bryce Canyon National Park and the Grand Canyon. It is a place where you can spend a few hours or a few days.

A word of caution is in order for families. On busy weekends, Coral Pink Sand Dunes is a popular area for three-wheelers, dune buggies and four-wheel drive outfits. This can create a dangerous situation because some of these recreational vehicles go over the sand dunes at a high rate of speed and may not see children playing in the sand. If you venture into the sand dune area with your kids, take a red flag or marker and keep close track of where the off-road vehicles are operating. If you don't want to worry, find an area that has been fenced to keep out vehicles and protect rare plants.

DEAD HORSE POINT — Located 34 miles northwest of Moab at the end of State Road 313, Dead Horse Point is one of those must-see places where there is a myriad of things for children to do.

Claret Cup   Simpson's Hedgehog   Beavertail

Cactus Flowers

Lizard

The Point itself rises 2,000 feet above the Colorado River and offers one of the finest views of the Colorado River and Upper Grand Canyon found anywhere in the Canyonlands Country. Yet, with steep cliffs on all sides of the 9,000-acre state park, it can be dangerous. Close supervision of children is necessary.

Dead Horse Point's 21 camping units fill up fast during busy spring and summer months. They have covered picnic tables, electrical hookups and sewage dump stations.

Kids always enjoy a self-guided nature trail and the one at Dead Horse Point introduces them to the deserts of Utah. When taking this easy one-fourth mile trail, children will learn about cliffrose, the pygmy forest, desert varnish, stone staircases, Mormon tea and other features of the desert. There are 5.5 miles of hiking trail within the park, much of it going along the rim of the canyon. A visitor center, open year round, has information on nearby areas as well as postcards, brochures, T-shirts, maps, posters and slide strips. Vending machines for snacks and drinks are also available. During the summer months, evening programs and ranger-guided walks are offered. Many are geared to children and can be enjoyed by the entire family.

ESCALANTE PETRIFIED FOREST – One mile west of the town of Escalante, east of Bryce Canyon National Park, Escalante Petrified Forest gives families the best of two worlds. It is an interesting natural area where children can learn about petrified wood and mineralized dinosaur bones by hiking along a guided nature trail near the campground.

The park, located on **Wide Hollow Reservoir,** can be used for fishing, waterskiing, or a cool swim off a primitive beach. When visiting the

Wide Hollow Reservoir at Escalante Petrified Forest State Park

Escalante area, with acres of Bureau of Land Management, state and national park, and U.S. Forest Service land nearby to explore, Escalante Petrified Forest is a good place to set up a base camp. It has a grassy campground that is ideal for tenters. The 21-unit facility has modern restrooms with showers, and plenty of room for kids to run and play. It is far enough away from the water that children won't have to be supervised constantly.

Escalante Petrified Forest State Park

GOBLIN VALLEY—Located off a narrow road 35 miles northwest of Hanksville, this remote natural area is hard to find—but worth the effort.

Though there are two formal hiking trails at Goblin Valley, its allure is its lack of structure. This is a park where children create their own trails and can hike where they please. The "goblins" which give the place its name can be seen by the dozens. Kids love to run loose among the goblins, letting their imaginations run wild as they perceive various animals, people and things in the eroded sandstone. My kids like to name each formation. There are also nearby sand dunes to explore.

The small 12-unit campground fills quickly during spring and fall holiday weekends and is oriented for trailers and motorhomes, although there are several secluded tent sites off the road that families should ask about. Hot showers in the restrooms make this a place where its all right for children to get dirty. The hikes into the valley can be short or long, depending on the endurance of your kids and the interest they show as soon as they walk into the valley.

GOOSENECKS OF THE SAN JUAN — Located near Natural Bridges National Monument in southwestern Utah, this ten-acre primitive park has few facilities or trails for families, though children might enjoy the spectacular view of the San Juan River Canyon where the river meanders back and forth, giving the overlook its name. There is an interpretive sign here explaining how the Goosenecks were formed. A path leads from the overlook to the ledges below. This path is unmaintained.

For people with children ten years of age or older, the nearby Honaker Trail is interesting. This historical trail was built by gold miners around the turn of the century for access from the canyon top to the river below. The trail is accessible from Utah Highway 16, the road to Goosenecks State Park. It is all on BLM land. Though the trail is not maintained, it is in remarkably good condition. The four-mile trail descends approximately 1,000 feet by traversing the canyon ledges, and hikers should have no trouble following it. Fossils can be found in the limestone formations crossing the trail. Ask at Natural Bridges or Edge of the Cedars State Park in Blanding for specific instructions on how to reach this trail.

Goosenecks of the San Juan State Park

GREAT SALT LAKE ANTELOPE ISLAND — When open, Antelope Island is a major tourist attraction providing hiking, swimming, beach activities and horseback riding in the beautiful setting of the Great Salt Lake.

Flooding of the Great Salt Lake has washed away the causeway to Antelope Island. Planning is continuing to determine a permanent use for Antelope Island.

For information on the island's current status, write to Antelope Island State Park, P.O. Box 618, Farmington, Utah 84025.

GREAT SALT LAKE STATE PARK, SALTAIR BEACH — One thing most visitors want to do when they get to Utah is visit the Great Salt Lake. This park, located 16 miles west of Salt Lake City, is designed to meet this demand.

The rising waters of the Great Salt Lake have closed a private recreational facility at Saltair. There is, however, a small sandy beach where families can swim and or enjoy a sunset picnic. A new boat ramp makes this a nice area for power boating or sailboating.

If you allow your children to swim in the Great Salt Lake, remember that the water is salty and, if they get it in their eyes, it's going to sting.

Like Antelope Island, visitors would do well to check on the current status of facilities before visiting Saltair Beach. Call the Salt Lake office of the Division of Parks and Recreation or write to Saltair Beach, P.O. Box 323, Magna, Utah 84044-0323.

Sea Gull / Utah State Bird

Saltair Beach at Great Salt Lake State Park

KODACHROME BASIN—In the midst of southern Utah's many tourist attractions, this small park is easy to overlook. That's a big mistake. Reaching the park can be intimidating because of a small stretch of dirt road. But unless it is raining hard, the road presents few problems. To find Kodachrome Basin, drive through Bryce Canyon National Park to the town of Tropic and continue until you get to Cannonville. Follow road signs from there.

The 24-unit campground is one of the most scenic in southern Utah. Modern restrooms, with showers, are available. The shaded campsites are located far from one another. Each has a picnic table, cement slab and barbecue grill. Firewood is furnished. A lighted group area is available.

There are five easy hikes within Kodachrome Basin. A self-guided nature trail points out numerous rocks and alcoves to hikers. My kids like the short trek to Shakespeare Arch, one of the most-recently discovered rock formations of this type in Southern Utah. The area, named Kodachrome Basin by the National Geographic Society because of its beautiful colors, is best known for its high, monolithic pinnacles. These are remnants of ancient freshwater springs.

A new horse riding concession at the park provides trail rides as well as surrey and stagecoach rides. The concessionaire caters to the disabled.

In close proximity are attractions like **Grosvenors Arch, Cottonwood Canyon, Bull Valley Gorge, Hackberry Canyon, Indian ruins**, the **Old Paria** ghost town and **Mossy Cave**. They can also be hiked with children.

Kodachrome Basin State Park

Early Morning at Kodachrome Basin State Park

Monument Valley

MONUMENT VALLEY — This state park is located in Monument Valley at the intersection of U.S. Highway 163 and the road to Oljeto and the Navajo Tribal Park. It is undeveloped and unsigned. Family travelers to this famous natural area might want to visit the **Navajo Tribal Park**. The Tribal Park includes a 17-mile unpaved loop road with eleven numbered scenic stops and a 100-unit campground. An entrance fee is often charged. If your children have watched any old westerns with you, they'll at least enjoy taking a short drive or hike through this area because it was the setting for many of these movies.

SNOW CANYON — This park, located five miles northwest of St. George, is open year-round, though it can get very hot in the summer. It is comfortable in the winter and early spring when most parks in Utah are still too cold to enjoy.

This park has much to offer children. The rock formations have a sandpaper texture which gives kids traction for rock scrambling. There are marked trails to lava caves as well as **West Canyon** and **Johnson's Arch**.

The 34-unit campground has trailer hookups with water and power, in addition to some tenting areas away from the recreation vehicle sites. If a family is tired of hiking, the one-acre lawn, horseshoe pits and basketball and volleyball facilities provide a diversion. A large, coral pink sand dune near the campground also should delight children.

There is a horseback and hayrack riding concession at Snow Canyon, giving still another family vacation option to visitors in "Utah's Dixie."

WASATCH MOUNTAIN — This large state park, located in the Heber Valley about an hour's drive from northern and central Utah, is the most heavily used park in the state's system, mainly because of its 27-hole golf course and camping facilities. It is particularly striking in the fall when the scrub oak changes color.

Giant Desert Hairy Scorpion

Because it is so popular, reservations for its 152-unit campground are a must. The campground has modern restrooms, showers and utility hookups. The nearby Chalet group area is available for activities like family reunions. Golf reservations are suggested, even during the middle of the week, when youngsters 17 and under get a $1.00 discount. Nearby private establishments offer horseback rentals and hot springs swimming. Wasatch Mountain State Park is open year-round.

This park is a hub for snowmobile and cross country ski activities on adjacent state and federal lands. Rentals for ski equipment and snowmobiles are available at the golf clubhouse.

The Historic Areas

ANASAZI INDIAN VILLAGE—This partially-excavated Indian village is off the beaten track but is worth visiting because children are fascinated with Indians. The staff here caters to families and takes the time to teach children about the Anasazi Indians. To find this park, drive east from Bryce Canyon National Park on State Highway 12, through Escalante, to the small town of Boulder. The park is just north of town.

Anasazi is a Navajo Indian word meaning "Ancient Ones." Archaeologists use it to describe the Basketmaker-Pueblo culture that existed from A.D. 1 to 1300 in the Four Corners plateau region of Colorado, New

Indian Remains at Anasazi State Park

94

Indian Pottery at Anasazi State Park

Mano and Metate at Anasazi State Park

Anasazi State Park

Mexico, Arizona and Utah. The partially excavated Indian village, though small, offers the opportunity to walk through an archaeological site and learn about the cultural heritage of this area.

When making the effort to visit this state park with children, use the self-guided trail brochure and study the remains of the pre-historic Indian village. You will be amazed at how many questions children will have about the village. In addition, a small museum at the park houses a collection of artifacts uncovered at the site.

Rangers give oral presentations to various school groups during the year. A few of these children return to give the same presentations to their parents. If you want to learn more about the ancient Indians on a family outing, get in touch with the Utah Natural History Museum at the University of Utah in Salt Lake City. The museum sponsors several trips a year to the Anasazi Indian Village where children and their parents become involved in archaeological excavations at the park and travel to nearby Indian ruins.

There is no campground here, though BLM, U.S. Forest Service and other state park camping areas are nearby. Group and individual picnic areas are available.

CAMP FLOYD AND STAGECOACH INN — Near the town of Fairfield about 50 miles southwest of Salt Lake City, this former military post quartered the largest troop concentration in the United States from 1858 to 1861. State park records show that 400 buildings housing 5,600 U.S. Army troops were located here. The troops were sent to the area to suppress an assumed Mormon rebellion that never materialized. Today, only a cemetery remains as evidence of this occupation.

Nearby Stagecoach Inn was an overnight stop on the historic overland stage and Pony Express route. It has been restored with original period furnishings and is open daily from March 15 to October 31.

Children can take a guided tour of the Stagecoach Inn Museum or Camp Floyd cemetery, and ranger-led talks can be arranged for those willing to make advance arrangements.

DANGER CAVE—This undeveloped state park, located one mile northeast of Wendover, was occupied by Indians about 10,000 B.C. While it may be worth a quick stop on a trip to Nevada or California, there is little here for children to see.

EDGE OF THE CEDARS—A State Heritage Park, 6.5 acres in size, Edge of the Cedars is located at the outskirts of Blanding City in south-western Utah. It is an interpretive area for families visiting nearby places like Newspaper Rock, Mesa Verde National Park, Hovenweep National Monument, Canyon de Chelly National Monument and Chaco Canyon National Monument in the Four Corners area. These areas have an ancient Indian theme. In the park is an Anasazi village built by pre-Columbian people. Part of this site was excavated in the late 1960s and early 1970s. Adjacent to the ruin is a museum building, containing two main exhibit halls that explain man's history in the Four Corners area. The displays present information on prehistoric people, contemporary Navajo and Ute

Excavation at Edge of the Cedars

98

Edge of the Cedars State Park Kiva

Indians, as well as the Anglo settlers of San Juan County. The museum houses one of the best exhibits of Anasazi pottery found in the Four Corners area.

The park is set up for self-guided tours. Particularly popular with children is a mano and metate where kids are invited to grind corn in the same manner as the Indians. A short walk takes visitors through the ruin complex located just behind the museum. A brochure gives information for each numbered post throughout the ruin. Children are permitted to climb down into the roofed kiva—an Indian ceremonial room—on a ladder through the roof. Also open for inspection in this area is a Navajo hogan (dwelling).

A botanical garden with a variety of plants indigenous to the area introduces children to desert ecology. A Navajo Indian garden of Indian corn and squash is planted in the traditional way each growing season.

While no camping is allowed in the park, there are picnic tables under Navajo sun shades. There is a Navajo Indian Arts and Crafts shop in the Museum, as well as a small book store. The park staff is knowledgeable about other Indian-related activities in the Four Corner's area.

FORT BUENAVENTURA—Located on a 32-acre tract of land in Ogden, this is the site of the mountain man fort established by Miles Goodyear in the early 1840s. It is believed to be the first permanent Anglo settlement in the Great Basin.

The park consists of stockade and cabin replicas on the original site and some picnic areas. The best time to visit Fort Buenaventura is during a rendezvous held by local mountain men or during other living history exhibitions where early skills and crafts are presented. Contact the park office or the Salt Lake office of the Division of Parks and Recreation for information on these activities.

FORT DESERET—Located nine miles southwest of Delta, this undeveloped state park has few facilities. However, its location makes it a good place to take a break during a long drive. The remains of an adobe and

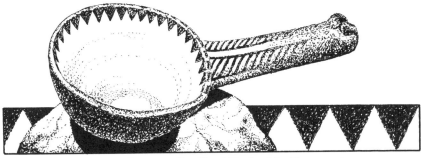

Indian Pottery Ladle / Probably Fremont

straw fort, 550-feet square by ten feet high are in evidence here. It was erected in 18 days by 98 men to protect local settlers against Indian raids during the Black Hawk War.

FREMONT INDIAN—One of the state's newest parks, Fremont Indian is located off the I-70 freeway southwest of Richfield. An interpretive center, with excellent hands on displays for children, presents the evolution of the Fremont Indian culture from A.D. 500 to 1300. Nature trails to Indian writings, a fine commercial concession which features horseback rides and evening programs and re-created Fremont homes are popular with children.

IRON MISSION—Located in Cedar City, this small park's museum and grounds tell the story of developing cultures in Iron County in the 1850s—when the Mormon prophet Brigham Young sent missionaries to develop iron resources needed by the settlers.

NEWSPAPER ROCK—Located twelve miles east on State Highway 211 from its junction with U.S. Highway 191, 15 miles north of Monticello, this ten-acre park is named for the native American petroglyph panel found here. The rock writings range from old to more recent times. They are only a short distance from the highway. A self-guided nature trail starting near the petroglyphs is one-fifth mile long. It gives children a good introduction to the Canyonlands country, especially if you plan to take them to the nearby Needles District of Canyonlands National Park.

While the campground is primitive—with pit toilets and no drinking water—it is attractive and a good alternative if Squaw Flat in Canyonlands is full, which it often is. Camping and admission are free.

PIONEER TRAIL—Coupled with Hogle Zoo, which is located across the street, Pioneer Trail State Park is one of the top tourist attractions for families in the Salt Lake Valley.

One of the major attractions is the "This Is the Place Monument," which when it was built in 1947, celebrated the 100th anniversary of the arrival of the Mormon pioneers in the Salt Lake Valley. A seven-minute audio presentation and three-wall mural portraying the 2,000-mile migration of Mormon pioneers can be viewed at the information center.

The monument itself is a small part of this ever-expanding state historical area.

A pioneer town called Old Deseret has been constructed north of the monument and a number of historical homes from Utah's pioneer era have been moved here. The town depicts life in pioneer Utah from the beginnings of settlement in 1847 until the coming of the railroad in 1869. Most of the buildings are authentic structures. The largest is the Brigham Young Forest Farmhouse, where guides take visitors on a tour of the home built by the famous Mormon prophet. My kids were impressed with the demonstration showing silkworms the pioneers imported to make their own silk. This farm home is open year-round, though hours are shorter during the winter

Newspaper Rock State Park

Newspaper Rock State Park

Rockport State Park

months. It's a good idea to give the historical area a phone call before traveling to it in the off-season.

Old Deseret includes a Blacksmith's Shop, some farm animals, an old Social Hall (which can be rented for family reunions) and a General Store with souvenirs. On some summer days, volunteers throughout Old Deseret recreate history. It's not unusual to see children learning how to make bricks, clothes, toys and candles in the old-fashioned way. A half-day can be spent here reading interpretive literature and walking through the town.

Perhaps the best time to take your children to Pioneer Trails State Park is on a holiday weekend. Pioneer Spring Days are celebrated on Memorial Day weekend; Pioneer Independence Day on July 4th; Pioneer Days of 1847 during the July 24th Days of 47 celebration; Pioneer Harvest Days on Labor Day weekend; and Pioneer Christmas during the first two weekends of December. Children get a chance to participate in pioneer games, taffy pulls, arts and crafts demonstrations and a variety of hands-on living history experiences.

UTAH FIELD HOUSE OF NATURAL HISTORY — Located in Vernal and sometimes called the Dinosaur Museum, this is a great place to visit with children, especially when you plan to drive a few miles farther to Dinosaur National Monument. Kids will enjoy the outdoor Dinosaur Garden which features 14 life-sized dinosaur replicas in a natural setting. Ancient fossil skeletal reproductions, archaeological and geological exhibits, fluorescent minerals and other natural history aspects of the Uinta Basin are also featured. A gift shop gives children a chance to purchase souvenirs such as replicas of old dinosaur bones, fossils or children's books.

The Water Parks

BEAR LAKE — Bear Lake, located on the Utah-Idaho border, is one of the most popular water recreation areas in Utah during the summer. Because of its popularity, getting camping reservations early for the 30-unit campground at the Bear Lake Marina or the 138-unit area at Rendezvous Beach is a must. There are 48 campsites with hookups for trailers at Rendezvous Beach. The sandy, gentle Rendezvous Beach and state-owned land on the east side of the lake at Cisco Beach provide public access to this natural lake. Facilities include showers and modern campgrounds. In the summer, kids might try their hands at picking fresh raspberries in nearby Garden City. There is a privately-operated waterslide, a golf course and boat and sailboat rentals available from several private marinas around the lake. Idaho also has state park facilities on the lake.

BIG SANDWASH — Located 14 miles northeast of Duchesne, this is a small reservoir with primitive camping facilities. If you want to introduce your children to trout fishing, try your luck here in the spring.

Waterskier Falls at Willard Bay

DEER CREEK — There are many things that make this close-to-the-Wasatch-Front reservoir in Heber Valley a desirable place for families. My children will remember it as the place they learned to fish. Yellow perch are abundant, especially on the upper end of the reservoir, and are even easy for young children to catch. They are good to eat but, most important, can be landed fast enough to hold a child's interest. Basic equipment with worms as bait will work very well at Deer Creek. The perch can also be caught through the ice in the winter.

Deer Creek's 23-unit campground tends to fill fast. There are some large beaches around the reservoir. Rainbow Bay is about one mile in length and has a gentle slope into the water. The Island area is 100 yards long and also has a gentle slope to the lake, but is often extremely crowded with sailboarders in the summer. Concessions are found around the reservoir that rent boats or sailing equipment.

EAST CANYON — Located near both Ogden and Salt Lake, this park receives heavy use by many Wasatch Front families. It has a 28-unit campground with a large grassy area and several covered picnic shelters for family reunions. The nearby beach, with a gentle slope into the reservoir, is a safe swimming area but is not roped and kids require supervision. The private marina rents waterski equipment, jet skis, paddleboats, canoes and fishing boats. My children like taking a paddleboat out.

Fishing is good from the shoreline in the fall and spring and through the ice in the winter, but tends to slow up during the summer when the water warms and power boaters tend to take over.

GREEN RIVER — Located in the southwestern Utah town of the same name, this underrated little park provides a base from which to see places like Arches National Park, the Book Cliffs or Goblin Valley State Park.

Boating at Willard Bay State Park

Camping, swimming and floating the river are the main activities at the park. Families with a raft or canoe might want to inquire about how to drive upstream and float down to the park.

The park has a modern 42-unit campground with showers. There is a large lawn area where football, volleyball, Frisbee and other lawn activities can be enjoyed. Many youth groups schedule gatherings here and a large barbecue grill is available for all groups. Runners like the park's jogging trail. Visit during "Melon Days" in early September to sample Green River's famous fruit. Park rangers hold a nightly slide program from May through September. Many of these programs are geared to children.

GUNLOCK—Located 16 miles northwest of St. George, Gunlock Reservoir is a 266-acre area. Its beach gives families a place to beat the heat in Utah's Dixie.

HUNTINGTON LAKE—This Emery County state park isn't well known among most family travelers in the state. There are beach facilities for wading and swimming and the water is warm in the summer. There are large lawn areas for various lawn games like croquet, badminton, volleyball or soccer. A picnic shelter can be reserved for family reunions. A 21-unit campground has flush restrooms and showers.

Waterskiing at a Utah State Park

HYRUM LAKE — This Cache County 3,000-acre reservoir is often crowded with local residents enjoying the swimming beach. Fishing is usually slow, but some boating is done here. The 36-unit campground has shade and grass.

JORDAN RIVER PARKWAY — The Jordan River Parkway winds its way through the Salt Lake Valley and is becoming an increasingly important greenspace in its urban setting. Along the river, there is a mix of state, county and city park developments with private facilities. The Raging Waters theme park, several golf courses and the Jordan Queen restaurant are just a few of the amenities.

The state has developed — and will develop more in the future — a series of jogging, bicycling and horse trails along the river. Kids like the bicycle motorcross park and model airplane airport. They can also learn to use off-road vehicles at a park designed for that use.

Major Salt Lake City parks like the Jordan Peace Gardens and Riverside Park, the state fairgrounds and several smaller green spaces developed and operated by the Division of Parks and Recreation provide family recreation areas in an urban environment. The Jordan River Parkway continues to grow in importance and eventually may be one of Salt Lake County's most impressive and well used family recreation areas.

LOST CREEK LAKE — This is a remote and difficult to reach reservoir because of a rough dirt road. It is located twelve miles northeast of Morgan in northern Utah. Facilities are primitive, but the lake is a good place to fish for trout, especially in the late spring and early fall.

MILLSITE LAKE — This Emery County park, located near the town of Ferron in central Utah, is still being developed but has excellent potential. It has two large picnic shelters and a 21-unit campground. There is a beach area with shallow water.

MINERSVILLE LAKE — Located twelve miles west of Beaver, this park, with a shaded 29-unit campground, is primarily used for fishing and boating. Trout fishing is often excellent here.

OTTER CREEK LAKE — Otter Creek, located four miles north of Antimony, is another park built primarily for fishermen angling for large trout. Fishing is good in the summer and winter. The lake is not far from Bryce Canyon National Park.

PALISADE LAKE — Located near the town of Sterling in Sanpete County, this lake is heavily oriented toward family recreation. It has a sandy beach for swimming and no motor boats are allowed on its surface, making it a perfect place to canoe or raft. Children under twelve are required to wear a life jacket on all waters in Utah. Palisade is stocked regularly with small rainbow trout.

Ice Fishing at Rockport State Park

Though children under ten are not allowed on the course, a nine-hole golf course provides another recreation opportunity. A hike around the reservoir follows an unmaintained 1.6-mile trail. Longer hiking trails — where game can often be viewed — are not far away.

Palisade has a modern 71-unit campground with showers and day-use facilities.

PIUTE LAKE — This undeveloped lake with primitive facilities is located near Marysvale. Fishing is on the upswing here, though still difficult. Rockhounding nearby is possible.

QUAIL CREEK — This relatively new reservoir near St. George promises to be a well-used addition to the state's recreation scene. It is oriented to boating and fishing. The Bureau of Land Management Dixie Red Cliffs facility is a few miles away.

ROCKPORT — Located four miles south of Wanship, Rockport is an important water-oriented park for thousands of Wasatch Front residents.

Fishing is best through the ice in the winter, when the reservoir is least crowded. Cross country skiers, snowshoers, and snowmobilers use more than 150 miles of adjacent roads and trails. Winter is also the best time to view wildlife. Observant children can see mule deer, elk, an occasional moose, chipmunks, golden and bald eagles, a variety of hawks, great horned owls, raccoons, Canada geese and many other kinds of waterfowl.

Rockport has nine campgrounds and more than 200 campsites. It is open year-round. Seven of the campgrounds are found on the east side of the lake with two others found below Wanship Dam along the Weber River. Some are nestled deep in trees while others are wide open on the beach or perched on cliffs overlooking the lake. Three campgrounds can be used for family reunions and groups. One has individual sites that can be reserved. The 36-unit campground — called Juniper — is the only one with modern restrooms and hot showers. It fills quickly in the summer.

Tubing at a Utah State Park

Tuber at Willard Bay

Boating at Willard Bay State Park

Motorboating, waterskiing, sailing and sailboarding are the most popular activities at Rockport. Families like the sandy beaches around the reservoir. Boat and sailboard rentals (with lessons) are available from a privately operated marina.

SCOFIELD — Scofield is one of the top family fishing areas in Utah and produces catches of rainbow and cutthroat trout year-round. Park rangers try to hold an annual kids fishing derby. The park is geared to fishing. There are two boat ramps and two campgrounds that generally fill on weekends from mid-spring until fall.

There are many backcountry trails here for hikers, horseback riders, cross country skiers and snowmobilers.

STARVATION — The camping and day-use facilities at Starvation, located four miles northwest of Duchesne in eastern Utah, were designed with families in mind. The day-use area contains a great deal of grass as well as a gently sloping, sandy beach. The 31-unit campground has an unusual playground constructed of logs. It has modern restroom facilities with hot and cold showers.

STEINAKER — Located seven miles north of Vernal, this reservoir is a good base for trips into the Uinta Basin to places like the State Fieldhouse of Natural History (a dinosaur museum), Flaming Gorge Reservoir and the Jones Hole Fish Hatchery. It has a 31-unit campground. There is fishing for trout and bass.

UTAH LAKE — This large natural lake, located west of Provo, was a fine family recreation area before recent floods damaged many of its facilities. A summer roller skating and winter ice skating rink are located here. Check with the park for hours. Kids can fish for white bass and small catfish, which are usually easy to catch. Limited camping is available near the visitor center.

WILLARD BAY — Located five miles north of Ogden, Willard Bay has two large marinas. The best one for family recreation is on the north. It has a large campground, a water slide, excellent boat launching facilities and picnic and beach areas close to the water. Because of its relatively low elevation, the water temperature is warmer than many of Utah's mountain lakes. Kids can fish for crappie year-round. The area is capable of hosting large crowds in the summer and often does.

YUBA RESERVOIR — Yuba Reservoir is a large body of water south of Nephi in central Utah with sandy beaches, boating, swimming, waterskiing, fishing and picnicking. Its low elevation makes it a warm boating area for spring, summer and fall. Though its small 19-unit campground fills early, there are many other spots around the lake to camp. Two group sites for family gatherings are also available. State park rangers are more than willing to answer questions about local history and folklore. Families might inquire about the Escalante and Dominguez Trail, the early Fremont Indian civilization, native plants and animals or how Yuba Dam was constructed.

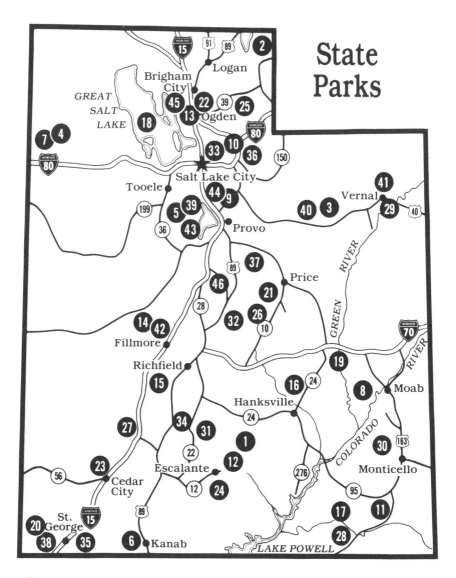

State Parks

GREAT SALT LAKE

Logan
Brigham City
Ogden
Salt Lake City
Tooele
Provo
Vernal
Price
Moab
Fillmore
Richfield
Hanksville
Monticello
Escalante
Cedar City
St. George
Kanab
LAKE POWELL

GREEN RIVER
COLORADO RIVER

1 ANASAZI		**6** CORAL PINK SAND DUNES
2 BEAR LAKE		**7** DANGER CAVE
3 BIG SAND LAKE		**8** DEAD HORSE POINT
4 BONNEVILLE SALT FLATS		**9** DEER CREEK LAKE
5 CAMP FLOYD		**10** EAST CANYON LAKE

Pelicans at Great Salt Lake

Uinta Mountains, Wasatch National Forest

CHAPTER FIVE

U.S. Forest Service Areas

It was just another Sunday afternoon at Payson Lakes Recreation Area in the Uinta National Forest.

Families spread out picnics on the grassy day-use area next to the small lake. Hot dogs were cooked on public barbecue grills. Though the water was chilly, many children and their parents swam delightedly.

Around the lake, people could be seen fishing. Others paddled canoes. Two young boys used the paved nature trail around the lake for a skate-board path.

At the nearby campground, outfits of all different styles were used by people escaping the city. There were tents, motorhomes, folks with horses and campers. Parents relaxed on lounge chairs and watched their children play tag. Enthusiastic groups used the volleyball court or softball diamond in the campground while others quietly played checkers on a picnic table.

Such scenes are common in most Utah national forest areas. In many ways, the small U.S. Forest Service campgrounds serve as parks and play areas for people in both the big cities along the Wasatch Front and the smaller communities around the state. It is no accident that during most years twice as many people visit northern Utah's Wasatch-Cache National Forest as Yellowstone National Park.

Every campground, nature trail and lake on these Forest Service lands has its own appeal.

The following covers only the highlights. For more details, you can contact the district ranger in the forest you plan to visit. The addresses for these offices are listed in the appendix of this book.

Wasatch-Cache National Forest

The Wasatch-Cache National Forest, located in northern Utah, is the home of 113 different recreation sites where families camp, ski, hike, snowmobile, picnic, fish and relax.

The forest begins at the Point of the Mountain on the Utah-Salt Lake County border and runs north to the Idaho border. It includes the canyon areas east of major Wasatch Front cities like Salt Lake City, Sandy, Bountiful, Ogden and Logan, as well as a portion of the Uinta mountain range. Part of the forest continues into Wyoming.

In many ways, these forest lands serve as urban parks. Families will find group-use areas in most of the six ranger districts (Ogden, Mountain View, Evanston, Kamas, Salt Lake and Logan) with facilities like volleyball courts and softball diamonds. The newer campgrounds cater to families by offering them double and triple sites with larger picnic tables.

The Wasatch-Cache National Forest is different from many other forests in the United States. It is used almost as often in the winter as other times of year. Families use the canyons for sleigh riding, snowmobiling, downhill and cross-country skiing. Some of the most famous ski resorts in America are located on Wasatch National Forest property.

Because of this heavy use, wise campers try to reach sites early. This is especially true of facilities along Utah Highway 150, commonly known as "The Mirror Lake Highway." Operated in part by the Kamas and Evanston ranger Districts, this section of the Wasatch-Cache National Forest becomes free of snow in mid-June and begins to get cold soon after Labor Day. In June, July and August the many campgrounds located along the highway fill fast. One of the big draws here is fishing the high mountain lakes that are surrounded by pines and verdant meadows. Families fish for

Amethyst Lake, Wasatch National Forest

Clark's Nutcracker

trout and camp near lakes like **Mirror, Butterfly, Lost, Lilly** and **Moosehorn**, stocked regularly by the Division of Wildlife Resources with easy-to-catch rainbows.

The Mirror Lake Highway area provides access to backpacking into the High Uintas Wilderness Area. Many families with young children may find these trails too long and too difficult. There are a number of short hikes for young children, however. I took my 18-month-old son Bryer into such an area just below Mirror Lake for his first backpacking experience. We walked only a mile and camped near a lake. Even on a busy holiday weekend, we were almost alone. For shorter hikes, check with the Kamas Ranger District office in the town of Kamas. The office usually is open on weekends.

In the winter, the Mirror Lake Highway is an important snowmobiling trail. The Division of Parks and Recreation regularly grooms the trail to Mirror Lake. The recently developed Beaver Creek ski trail is gentle enough for novice cross country skiers.

The **Salt Lake Ranger District** is east of Utah's capital city and provides a canyon setting and urban recreation area. It is a rare family that fails to visit the "canyons" at least once a year.

Mill Creek is one popular day use canyon. It has no developed overnight campgrounds, but it does have dozens of picnic sites. It contains trailheads for numerous hikes and, in the winter, the road is blocked to eliminate snowmobile and four-wheel drive traffic. This makes it a convenient place to teach children how to cross country ski. It is where my kids learned to ski at the age of five. It is a children's winter paradise.

There are two guided nature trails in the Salt Lake Ranger District, though both are in need of repair. Guide booklets for the one-fourth mile **Brighton Nature Trail** in **Big Cottonwood Canyon** and the one-half mile **Mueller Park Picnic Area** trail east of Bountiful are available at the Salt

Raccoons

120

Hiking in a National Forest

Visitor on Aspen Leaf

Lake Ranger District Office at 6944 South 3000 East. There are times when the booklet can be found near trailheads, but more often than not, they have been taken by other hikers. These trails are good for introducing young children to hiking. The booklets emphasize the names of plants and trees in the area and children who know the names of the natural things they find in the forest make those things their friends.

The Salt Lake Ranger District lists 15 easy hikes, most of which are suitable for families, although younger children may not be able to complete the longer ones. To determine how far your child can go, start with short distances and go farther each time.

The Salt Lake Ranger District and many commercially-produced trail guide booklets have more detailed information on these hikes.

Major recreation sites and campgrounds are found in Big and Little Cottonwood Canyons, Farmington Canyon, South Willow Canyon and the Mueller Park area east of Bountiful.

The **Ogden Ranger District** begins north of Farmington where the Salt Lake District ends. One of the major recreation areas in this district is **Pine View Reservoir**, a summer boating, fishing, swimming and camping area.

There are numerous hikes in the Ogden Ranger District, but many of them are difficult. Two of the easier hikes are the one-mile **Skintoe Trail** on the north end of **Causey Dam** and the 3.2-mile **Skullcrack Trail** on the south end of **Causey Dam**. Park near the Boy Scout camp and cross the dam to the east before hiking south. On the other side of Causey Dam is the trailhead for the 3.2-mile Skullcrack Trail, at the south end of the dam. First-time hikers and their parents will enjoy the forest scenery around the

Hiking in a U.S. National Forest in Utah

reservoir. There is a small dispersed camping site at the end of the trail. The only other access is by canoe. Older children might want to try the .8-mile trek to Waterfall Canyon that begins at the top of 29th street in Ogden. Hikers can view the colorful wildflowers on the way to the waterfall. Watch out for rattlesnakes on this trail.

Information on these trails and recreation sites can be obtained at the Ogden Ranger District headquarters in the Ogden Federal Building at 324 25th Street.

The **Logan Ranger District** has some informative interpretive trails and some easily accessed campgrounds. Three self-guided nature trails—the two-mile **Riverside Trail**, the **Tony Grove Trail** and the **Limber Pine Nature Trail**—will help children and adults learn about the ecology of the forest. The Limber Pine and Tony Grove Lake trail guides were produced in cooperation with the Bridgerland Audubon Society and feature lists of common birds, wildflowers, trees and shrubs your family might see in this forest. Families with young children often enjoy fishing for easy-to-catch rainbow trout at **Third Dam Impoundment** and **Tony Grove Lake**, stocked regularly by the Division of Wildlife Resources. For information, contact the Logan Ranger District Office at 910 South Highway 89-91 in Logan.

The least visited ranger districts in the Wasatch-Cache National Forest are the **Mountain View** and **Evanston Ranger Districts**. Located in Wyoming, much of the land they manage is in Utah. These areas are less crowded. **Bridger Lake, Marsh Lake** and **China Meadows** in the Mountain View District all have quiet campgrounds and family fishing, rafting and canoeing opportunities. There are many campgrounds in the Evanston District, which is comprised of the northern portion of the Mirror Lake

Nordic Skiing on Wasatch National Forest (Photo by Tom Wharton)

Glacier Walking on Bald Mountain Trail, Wasatch National Forest

Highway. One of the better trails is the two-thirds mile trek to **Ruth Lake**. The hike begins on the Mirror Lake Highway at an elevation of 10,120 feet and continues to a small lake at 10,360 feet. The trail itself is well defined and not difficult, even for very young children. In the Ruth Lake area, there are four lakes that contain fish and are within one mile of Ruth Lake. There are no marked trails to these lakes but, with a map, they are not difficult to discover. The terrain is relatively easy to hike, making this a good spot for a family backpacking trip.

Fishlake National Forest

The Fishlake National Forest Headquarters are in Richfield. Its ranger districts are in Fillmore, Loa, Beaver and Richfield. Many of the canyon areas included in this central Utah forest are relatively small and remote, though they provide family camping and fishing opportunities.

Perhaps the best known U.S. Forest Service facility in this area is **Fish Lake**. Located 25 miles southeast of Richfield, this 2,600-acre lake at about 8,800 feet elevation is surrounded by tall pines and rugged mountains. Cabin and boat rentals in addition to public campground facilities, make it busy during the summer. Fishing from boats on the east side of Fish Lake is best. My family has found more accessible and easier fishing opportunities on the shoreline of **Johnson Reservoir,** located just up the road from Fish Lake. A 1.4-mile long asphalt surface trail runs parallel with Fish Lake and has been designated a National Recreation Trail. Trailheads are found at the Bowery Haven and Fish Lake lodges on either end of the lake. Watch for an occasional bald eagle or frequent visits by osprey. A self-guided auto tour of geologic features within the Fish Lake Basin is available to people who pick up the pamphlet at Forest Service offices in Richfield or Loa. Campgrounds at Fish Lake are usually occupied by Thursday evening so visitors who plan to camp over the weekend should plan on getting there early in the week or early in the day.

Mule Deer

As in many of the forest service areas away from the Wasatch Front, a family can find relative solitude when visiting the Fishlake National Forest even in developed areas. You might try a trip to **Indian Creek**, located ten miles north of Beaver, or to **Manderfield Reservoir**. A two-mile long trail begins north of the reservoirs. You can view Beaver and Piute counties from either side of the ridge on this hike.

Thousand Lake Mountain, located nine miles east of Loa, has camping, fishing and hiking. A six-mile (round trip) trail to **Neff Lake** is relatively easy. **Bullion Canyon**, five miles east of Marysvale, shows evidence of mining activity. A trail on **Pine Creek** leads to a 40-foot waterfall. The trail starts from the road on the north side of the creek and traverses the canyons. The waterfalls are about one-half mile up the trail and off the main route. See if your kids can hear them before they come into view.

There are 32 developed recreation sites on the Fishlake National Forest, all suitable for family recreation. A map of the area is available at any of the ranger district offices.

Ashley National Forest

The Ashley National Forest is located in the northeastern part of Utah and, because of its remoteness, is less crowded than the canyon areas along the Wasatch Front. It has 68 developed recreation sites, though many of them are located in the Flaming Gorge Ranger District of the Flaming Gorge National Recreation Area. Information on that family recreation destination is provided in the National Recreation Area chapter of this book.

There are several areas in the **Flaming Gorge Ranger District** that, although not a part of the national recreation area, are worthy places for family vacations. The **Sheep Creek** geological drive west of Flaming Gorge takes visitors on a trip through bizzare multi-hued geologic layers. It leads to small lakes with campgrounds and fishing like **Browne, Sheep Creek** and **Spirit**. There are some short day hikes into the High Uintas Wilderness Area out of Spirit Lake. When the lodge is operating at Spirit Lake, horse and cabin rentals also are available.

There are plenty of recreational opportunities in the other three ranger districts of the Ashley National Forest, including the Vernal, Roosevelt and Duchesne areas.

The **Whiterocks Campground** on the Vernal District is situated near some unique geologic features, a stream and numerous beaver ponds. The **Lodgepole Campground** is one of the most developed in the Ashley Forest. It has such extras as electricity and flush toilets. It is close to Flaming Gorge and fills to capacity on major holidays and most weekends. About five

Rocky Mountain Bighorn Sheep

miles from the Lodgepole Campground is the **Stringham Cabin Historic Site** in **East McKee Meadow**. Turn at the sign saying Winterhawk and then drive to within 200 yards of the rustic cabin, once used as a base camp by sheepherders. An interpretive sign explains the history of the area. One possible day hike in this district leads to **Chepeta Lake** on the eastern half of the **Highline Trail**. The Highline trail can take hikers all over the High Uintas Primitive Area.

Families looking for rustic cabins, boat, and horseback rentals and a small lodge might visit **Moon Lake,** located above Mountain Home in the Lake Fork Drainage on the **Roosevelt Ranger District.** My father took me to Moon Lake for my first overnight fishing trip when I was 12, and I've had a soft spot for it ever since. While the water is too cold for swimming, boaters and anglers can explore the pine-covered shores of the lake. There is a developed campground near the lodge. The **Brown Duck Trail** is a day hiking area for families looking to spend a few hours in the wilderness. The **Yellowstone** area in the Roosevelt Ranger District also has several campgrounds. Horses are for rent at the dude ranch near the end of the road in Uinta Canyon. Guests can go on pack trips from here. There are some hikes in this area, though most may be too difficult for young children.

In the **Duchesne Ranger District**, work is being completed on the **Stillwater Dam**. A one-mile nature trail will surround this new reservoir. When the dam is completed in the spring of 1988, many new campgrounds will be constructed along **Rock Creek** where there is a small lodge. The **North Fork of the Duchesne** is a famous stream. This is a good place for children to try fly fishing because of the lack of brush along the banks. The streams are stocked all summer. There are campgrounds here and **Defas Dude Ranch** on the North Fork rents horses and cabins.

Uinta National Forest

Some of Utah's most important national forest family recreation sites are found on the Uinta National Forest. This forest is located east of heavily-populated Utah County. It includes the important **Strawberry-Soldier Creek-Currant Creek** recreation complexes east of Heber City. Major new campground complexes, complete with specially designed units that accommodate large families and groups — have recently been finished at **Payson Lakes, Strawberry Reservoir** and **Currant Creek Reservoir**. A reservation system makes it possible to reserve an individual or group spot up to one year in advance on ten Uinta National Forest campgrounds. **Blackhawk** and **Currant Creek Campgrounds** even have specially designed facilities for families with horses. For information on the reservation system, contact the Uinta National Forest headquarters at 88 West 100 North in Provo.

One new family-oriented facility is the campground at **Currant Creek Reservoir**. This is a fun place for campers with young children to make their initial foray into the woods. The site has a self-guiding nature trail describing natural resource management activities, the Central Utah Project and identifies animals and plants. Several playground structures for children are found in a sandy "tot lot" on Loop D. The facility has flush toilets, a trailer dump station and a boat ramp and is adjacent to Currant Creek Reservoir, which is stocked regularly with trout. Currant Creek is a cut above the average public campground and is large enough to accommodate a crowd.

There are several other family recreation sites in the **Heber Ranger District**. In **Daniels Canyon**, the **Whiskey Springs Picnic Area** is a day-use only facility. It has a plant-identification nature trail, a wooden play structure and vault toilets. The **Mill Hollow Campground**, located east of Woodland, is more rustic, but is a popular alpine fishing area. Hiking trails out of Daniels Canyon include **Dry Canyon, Clegg Canyon, Center Canyon, Row Bench** and **Thornton Hollow**. Many of these trails may be a bit steep for young children. For families who like to fish, the huge campgrounds at the now combined   Strawberry-Soldier Creek Reservoir

Tibble Fork Reservoir, Uinta National Forest

Cascade Springs, Uinta National Forest

complex are plentiful and have running water, flush toilets and covered picnic tables. Boat rentals are available at marinas at both Strawberry and Soldier Creek.

On the **Spanish Fork Ranger District**, the best family-oriented areas are the **Payson Lakes** complex and the nearby **Blackhawk** group-use campground. There is a nature trail surrounding the small reservoir east of Payson, Payson Lake. There is a sandy beach, grassy picnic area and some fine picnic spots here. The campground is large, well maintained and well supervised. The Blackhawk facility has accommodations for horses and can be reserved for big reunions. Several hiking trails on the district are: the **Cottonwood, Jocks Canyon, Dry Canyon Ridge Trail, Wadsworth Canyon Trail, Maple Canyon, Spanish Fork Peak Trail, Fifth Water Trail** and **Nebo Bench Trail.** Some of these are quite long with steep elevation gains, so families might want to get more information from the Spanish Fork Ranger District Office at 44 West 400 North in Spanish Fork.

One of the most interesting of these trails is the **Fifth Water Trail** in **Diamond Fork Canyon**. Hike from **Three Forks** to a foot bridge and follow **Sixth Water Creek** up a moderate tree-shaded trail. At 1.1 miles, a bridge crosses the creek where the trail forks. To the left is **Sixth Water** and to the right **Fifth Water.** Following Fifth Water Creek up an easy-to-moderate grade, a hiker passes numerous pools and small rapids. Fifth Water is noted for its warm sulfur springs, the odor of which is evident along much of the trail. A popular stopping point is located about 1.5 miles up Fifth Water near a waterfall. One of the larger hot springs is found here too. this is a

U.S. National Forest in Utah

Horseback Riding, U.S. National Forest

Hiker Paul Fadus in Uinta National Forest

nice place for a swim, so bring your suits. The paved **Nebo Loop Drive**, with access from Payson, Santaquin Canyon and Nephi, is clothed in reds, oranges and yellows in the fall.

The major recreation site on the **Pleasant Grove Ranger District** is the **Tibble Fork-Silver Flat Reservoir** complex in the **North Fork of American Fork** canyon. Both small reservoirs are stocked with trout and are quite busy. Tibble Fork has a large campground. The entrance to **Timpanogos Cave National Monument** (see National Monuments chapter) is also in American Fork Canyon. The scenic **Alpine Loop** connects Provo and American Fork Canyons and takes a driver past the **Sundance Ski Resort**. It is a common favorite of family drives, especially in the fall. When taking that drive, take the short drive to the **Cascade Springs Interpretive Trail**, which is a good place to introduce very young children to hiking. This high-developed trail is found by driving 6.5 miles on paved roads from the crest of the Alpine Loop. The short (.6 mile) walk takes less than 20 minutes over a paved and boardwalk path where a person can spend hours enjoying the rushing waters or watching the trout dart through the pools. Cascade Springs consists of a number of springs producing over seven million gallons of water daily, flowing over a series of travertine ledges and through a series of pools. Signs along the trail inform your children about springs and their origin. There are no picnic facilities are available. My children love to try and find the trout in the clear waters of Cascade Springs, and I think this is one of the premier nature trails in the state. Other possible hikes in the area include the **Stewart Cascades Trail, Silver Lake Trail, Rock Canyon Trail, Pittsburgh Lake Trail, Forest Lake Trail** and **Big Baldy Trail**. Many of those are quite short and suitable for younger children. For detailed information on these hiking trails, contact the Pleasant Grove Ranger District office at 390 North 100 East in Pleasant Grove.

Manti-LaSal National Forest

Located in the east central and southeastern mountain areas of Utah, the appeal of the Manti-LaSal National Forest lies in its remoteness. There are developed campgrounds in this part of the state but they receive relatively low visitation. This is especially true in the extreme southeastern corner in the Moab and Monticello Ranger Districts. The campgrounds here are located only a few miles from places like Canyonlands National Park and Arches National Park. While they offer relief from the desert's summer heat, many families are unaware they exist.

The **Monticello Ranger District** has campgrounds that service over 35 hiking trails, several suitable for young children. One is a self-guiding loop trail which begins in the **Devils Canyon Campground**, takes less than 30 minutes to travel. After helping children identify a number of forest plants, the trail leads to a small Moki Indian ruin. Another hike recommended for families is the **Arch Canyon Trail**, a continuation of another trail starting on lands administered by the Bureau of Land Management. A BLM sign on Interstate 95, one mile west of **Comb Ridge**, marks the road that leads to Arch Canyon. The mouth of the canyon is 2.5 miles up that road. The trail starts out as an old jeep road that winds its way up the canyon, frequently crossing the creek. There are several arches, hanging gardens and some cliff dwellings visible in the canyon. This trail is 12 miles long and might be the place to introduce kids to backpacking. For information, contact the Monticello Ranger District at 406 East Central.

The LaSal Mountains, which can be seen from Arches National Park and are located near Moab, are among the least visited of all Utah's national forest lands. Many of the 18 hiking trails on the **Moab Ranger District** are suitable for children though some are rarely used. A **LaSal Mountain Trail Guide** describing these trails and their difficulty can be picked up at the Moab Ranger District office at 446 South Main in Moab. There are two developed campgrounds in this part of the forest. A paved loop drive that connects State Highway 128 with U.S. 1919 can be taken to get a view of Arches National Park's slickrock from across the Colorado River.

One of the most developed recreation sites on the Manti-LaSal National Forest is the **Joe's Valley Reservoir** campground complex located west of Orangeville on State Highway 29. The reservoir is stocked regularly with trout. The bank fishing was fast enough to maintain my kids' attention. A large campground with flush toilets and a marina with boat rentals and a small cafe comprise this uncrowded recreation center. There are two quiet campgrounds and a number of good fishing areas on Highway 31 that connects Fairview with the town of Huntington. We especially like the one at **Boulger Canyon** near the heavily stocked small **Boulger Reservoir**. It can be crowded on weekends.

The major attraction on the **Ferron Ranger District** is **Ferron Reservoir**, high in the **Manti Mountains** between the towns of Mayfield in Sanpete County and Ferron in Emery County. The season here is relatively short – usually limited to July, August and September – and the small campground is often full. A rustic lodge with boat, cabin, and horseback rentals is also available.

The most popular family recreation site in the **Sanpete Ranger District** is the **Manti Community Campground** east of Manti. Families flock here in the summer when the **Mormon Miracle Pageant** is held at the **Manti Temple** close by.

136

Death Hollow, Dixie National Forest

Dixie National Forest

Located amid the splendor of famous national parks like Bryce Canyon National Park and Zion National Park and the beauty of Lake Powell, the Dixie National Forest is too often missed by travelers anxious to see the better-known attractions. It is an alternative camping area and recreation spot.

There, for example, is a campground in the **Powell Ranger District** along State Highway 12 that could best be described as the gateway to Bryce Canyon National Park. It is named **Red Canyon**. The rock formations are similar to those seen at Bryce. A short nature trail here is an introduction to what visitors will see later. The campground is an alternative to the National Parks in the busy summer when they are full.

One of the major areas in the **Cedar Ranger District** is the **Panguitch Lake** area. This is a highly-developed reservoir famous for its fishing. Several lodges that have boat rentals are found around the reservoir. Other family areas can be found near State Highway 14 in **Cedar Canyon** at both **Navajo Lake** and **Duck Creek**. There are privately-owned lodge facilities at both spots. Navajo Lake has some developed U.S. Forest Service campgrounds, though they are quick to fill in the summer. On the **Cedar Ranger District**, some possible family hiking trails include the **Cascade Falls Trail**, a short one-half mile hike; the **Bristlecone Pine Trail**; the **Lava Desert**, and the **Ice Cave**. With adult supervision children can explore **Mammoth Cave**, a lava tube formed by a volcano. For information on the trailheads to these areas, contact the Cedar City Ranger District at 82 North 100 East; Cedar City, Utah.

The **Boulder Mountain** area of the Dixie National Forest, which includes both the **Teasdale** and **Escalante Ranger Districts**, is a forested island oasis in the midst of the desert. A number of short hikes lead to lakes where hungry brook trout lurk. There are several developed and non-developed campsites along the recently paved Boulder to Grover road. Some of these campgrounds are a less crowded alternative to the campground at Capitol Reef National Park, which fills nearly every night during the summer. Many fishermen like the campground at **Lower Bowns Reservoir.**

The **Pine Valley Ranger District** in the extreme southeastern part of Utah northwest of St. George, is one of the lesser known forest service areas in Utah. It has two campgrounds high enough to beat the scorching heat of Utah's Dixie during the summer. There are several short hikes to be found here.

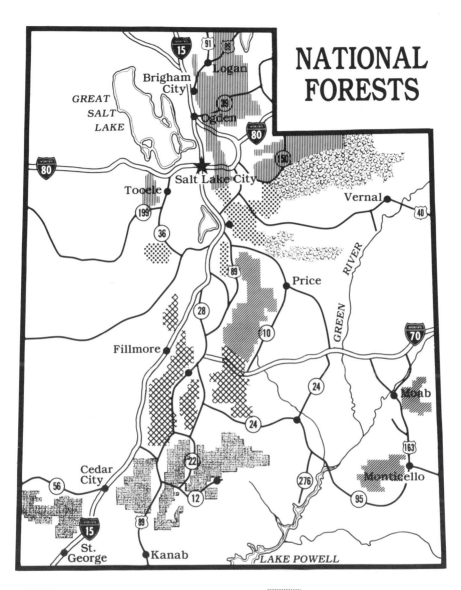

NATIONAL FORESTS

 ASHLEY
NATIONAL FOREST

 DIXIE
NATIONAL FOREST

 FISHLAKE
NATIONAL FOREST

 MANTI-LA SAL
NATIONAL FOREST

 UINTA
NATIONAL FOREST

 WASATCH-CACHE
NATIONAL FOREST

Fisher Towers

CHAPTER SIX

Bureau of Land Management Areas

As is our family's custom, the vacation started in the early morning darkness. It was possible to see the Milky Way as the van crept along the remote western Utah desert road in silence.

Then, as the eastern sky began to light up, we turned west on a lonely paved road off U.S. Highway 6 and 50, 22 miles west of Nephi. We drove toward the **Little Sahara Recreation Area.** *This, we reasoned, looked like an interesting place to eat breakfast and allow the children to discover the wild desert playground.*

We drove to the **Jericho Picnic Area.** *Even in the summer, when the temperatures at this 60,000-acre recreation area of sagebrush flats, juniper-covered hills and free moving sand dunes can reach 100 degrees, the morning breeze was cool. The wind blew the breakfast dishes from the table and the kids had to chase them to keep from littering. On a spring or fall weekend, the picnic area would be full of happy people. This summer morning, however, it was empty. We had it to ourselves.*

Little Sahara is one of the few areas in Utah where families have virtually unlimited use of the land for their dune buggies, dirt bikes and three and four-wheel vehicles. On Easter weekend, as many as 10,000 people converge on this area and jam its four developed recreation areas. Developed camping sites include the 41-unit Jericho Picnic area, the 84-unit **Oasis Campground** *and the 50-unit* **White Sands Campground.** *These three sites have flush toilets and water. Even the* **Sand Mountain** *area, with no camping units but 300 parking stalls, portable restrooms and water will fill on this busy weekend. The facilities and the sand combine to make this one of Utah's best off-road vehicle areas.*

But our family did not have a dirt bike or a three-wheeler. A fenced sand play area near the picnic area — where off-road vehicles are not allowed — provided a perfect place to explore the sand and listen to the quiet.

The sand dunes looked deserted but, in the early morning before the wind swirled and moved the fine sand, before dozens of happy children turned it into a haven for making castles, there were some things to examine carefully. Were those rabbit tracks in the sand? They came to a sudden end. And, what of the insect tracks? Where would they lead? These were mysteries.

After a long morning drive 115 miles from home in Salt Lake City, we'd found a giant playground. It was a place to climb a tall dune and then roll down. It was a spot where kids could hold hands and leap off a mountain of sand with a soft landing assured. It was an area where Dad and Mom could lay down and be buried with only their heads showing. It was a place where a kid could be a kid.

Like the Bureau of Land Management's other 17 developed recreation sites in Utah, it takes some effort to get to the Little Sahara Recreation Area. There is a wild, primitive feeling about these lands. Amazing in their diversity, the BLM lands are often more remote than the national parks or the national forests. They possess a spirit of their own.

Take, for example, the **Calf Creek Recreation Area** located 15 miles east of **Escalante** on Utah Highway 12. There is a small ten-unit campground plus group area. Spring comes early here and, after a long cold winter, Calf Creek can be a breath of fresh air. Children enjoy nothing better than wading in the shallow stream made warm by the sun. **Calf Creek Falls** is the major attraction within the Calf Creek Recreation Area. The **Lower Falls** are accessible by a 2.75-mile trail, most of which is in the sand. The falls plunge into a dark emerald-green pool. This is a long trail for young children, but if you take your time and plan a full day, there is much you can see along the way. A trail guide, which points out such things as Indian ruins, a miniature arch, petroglyphs and the names of common plants in the area, will help keep the kids interested in the hike. Be aware that the campground at Calf Creek fills up fast and can be a difficult place to get campsites, especially on busy spring.

The **Devils Garden Outstanding Natural Area** is located along the **Hole-in-the-Rock Road** about 19 miles southeast of Escalante. The facilities consist of three picnic tables, a graveled access road, parking area and pit toilets. No water is available. In this natural setting is a small collection of the sandstone formations found throughout southern Utah. There are arches, bridges, and windows. The pedestal-shaped formations look similar to those at Goblin Valley State Park. My children had a hard time leaving this natural playground. The Escalante area has a number of more difficult hikes. Information on these trails for the more adventurous soul is available from the BLM office in the town of Escalante.

An unusual Bureau of Land Management recreation site is the **Cleveland-Lloyd Dinosaur Quarry**, located 15 miles east of the Emery County town of Cleveland (and 35 miles south of Price) in southeastern Utah. Hours at the Quarry often change, so check with the state office of the BLM in Salt Lake City or with the nearby BLM office in Price before making the drive. Some 10,000 bones—including many of the world's most famous dinosaur fossils displayed in museums throughout the world—have been excavated here. They represent about 100 different specimens. More than 30 skeletons have been assembled from these bones. At the quarry there is a visitor center, quarry exhibit, as well as restrooms and picnic tables.

The **Cedar Mountain** and **San Rafael** facilities are found in the vicinity of the dinosaur quarry. The Cedar Mountain site, usually open from April to November, is 16 miles southeast of Cleveland and has ten picnic units but no drinking water. The San Rafael Campground, located 25 miles southeast of Cleveland, is a relatively primitive facility that does have drinking water. Though small (eleven units) and relatively primitive, it is an acceptable area for families who enjoy using off-road vehicles. The season is long, usually running from March through November.

The BLM's three **Henry Mountain Recreation Areas—Lonesome Beaver, McMillan Spring** and **Starr Spring**—are remote and have been closed at times in past years due to federal budget cuts. The Starr Spring Campground, located 50 miles southwest of Hanksville, is surrounded by a

BLM: Devils Garden

143

Moab Slickrock Trail (Photo by Tom Wharton)

Pelican Lake

juniper forest. It is an alternative to the Bullfrog Campground at nearby Lake Powell.

Also in the Price area is **Price Canyon Campground**, located 15 miles north of Price on U.S. Highway 50 and 6 and three miles west. This is popular locally but has a relatively short season. Facilities include 18 camping units, 12 picnic areas, toilets and drinking water.

The **Dixie Red Cliffs Recreation Area** is located north of St. George on the I-15 frontage road near Leeds. This campground has water, is open year round and is often full. It's a good place for a winter family camping trip. Because of the drop-offs, you'll want to keep an eye on your children. An easy one-half mile nature trail (a trail booklet is available) will introduce your family to a variety of desert plants and tell how they were used by pioneers and Indians.

The BLM also manages campgrounds at two Utah fishing areas. **Baker Reservoir**, located 24 miles north of St. George via Utah Highway 18, is primarily a trout fishery. Bank fishing with bait works well here. The campground is situated away from the water in a juniper forest. **Pelican Lake**, located in eastern Utah 15 miles west of Vernal on U.S. 40, is known for its warmwater fishing for large bluegill. These are easy to catch, especially in the spring. Children might also study and identify some of the birds in the marsh-like wetlands which surround Pelican Lake. Yellow-headed blackbirds are particularly noisy and plentiful in the spring.

The **Canyon Rims** complex located 22 miles north of Monticello on U.S.-163 is a good overflow area for Canyonlands National Park and Arches National Park. Water is available at both the **Hatch Point** and **Windwhistle** campground facilities. Space is almost always available. The vastness of Canyonlands National Park is revealed from the **Anticline** and **Needles Overlooks.**

The **Fisher Towers**, located 20 miles northeast of Moab, have been the site of more than 20 movies and two spectacular automobile television commercials filmed in 1964 and 1974. There is a small picnic area with a view of the towers, some of which are 900 feet high. Perhaps the best way to see the area is to hike the 2.2-mile trail, which takes about three to four hours to complete. Be sure to take water, especially in the summer.

Located near the Moab BLM office is the **Moab Slickrock Bike Trail.** Originally built for motorcycles, it is now being used by mountain bikers. I took my eleven-year-old daughter and ten-year-old twin sons on the 2.3-mile practice loop on the petrified sand dunes. They used their BMX-style bicycles while my wife and I rented mountain bikes from a shop in Moab. There is an advanced 10.3-mile main loop trail and a few side trails. There are several scenic overlooks including views of **Updraft Arch** and **Shrimp Rock**, but the thrill is either biking or hiking the petrified sand dunes. Because of the drop-offs, it is important to closely supervise your children.

Moving closer to the Wasatch Front, many off-road vehicle enthusiasts and history buffs enjoy following the **Pony Express Trail** through the west desert to **Simpson Springs**, 25 miles west of Vernon on a graveled county road. If you want to teach your children about the history of the Pony Express, you might want to pick up a trail brochure at the BLM's Salt Lake District office at 2370 South 2300 West. This guide will give you a map of the dirt road in one of Utah's most remote areas. It will show you how to reach the **Faust Junction, Simpson Springs, Boyd Station** and **Canyon Station** interpretive sites. This is a 300-mile round trip. There is a campground, with water, located at Simpson Springs, where a restored Pony Express station still stands. The **Fish Springs National Wildlife Refuge** is a good place to take children bird watching. And, the rugged **Deep Creek Mountains** to the west are a good place for a primitive camping experience.

This isn't an area for families seeking highly developed accommodations. In fact, there are no gas stations, grocery stores or commercial facilities along the entire route. Still, my children enjoyed the bird refuge, liked seeing the desert wildlife and gained some first-hand knowledge of what a Pony Express rider may have experienced on his trip through this desolate country. Look closely and you might be fortunate enough to see an illusive coyote.

The BLM also manages portions of the Green and Colorado Rivers. For families looking for a river trip, **Labyrinth Canyon** on the **Green River** (below the town of the same name) is often used for flat-water canoe trips. Either shuttle cars between **Green River State Park** and **Mineral Canyon** on the **Dead Horse Point State Park** road or hire a commercial outfitter in Moab to shuttle you and your equipment back. There are no rapids or whitewater on this stretch, which is particularly calm in late August and early September.

There are a number of other smaller BLM-managed areas in the state which, while they may not be worth a special trip, can enhance your family's vacation when traveling to other areas. Examples of these are the **John Jarvie Historic Property** and the **Drive Through the Ages** in northeastern Utah, near Flaming Gorge National Recreation Area. The Jarvie Historic Property, located near **Brown's Park** along the Green River, is open from 8:00 a.m. to 5:00 p.m. from May to October. It gives visitors a glimpse of turn-of-the-century frontier life in what is still a remote part of the west. The ranch includes a store, post office, river ferry and cemetery.

A brochure for the Drive Through the Ages can be picked up at the Vernal office of the BLM. This 30-mile interpretive drive on Utah Highway 44 between Vernal and Flaming Gorge includes stops that explain the changes in geologic time along the way—by pointing out the differences in the rock formations. The **Hog Springs Picnic Area**, located 37 miles southeast of Hanksville on Utah Highway 95, is a roadside facility with fireplaces, tables, toilets and drinking water. There are numerous side canyons where families can take short hikes. Nearby is a natural rock alcove with Indian pictographs, including a drawing called the **Moki Queen**. A large number of Indian rock writing can be observed at the **Parowan Gap Indian Petrograph Site**, located 12 miles northwest of the town of Parowan in Iron County. The **Ponderosa Grove** campground near the **Coral Pink Sand Dunes** is a possible camping alternative when the state park facility is full.

In addition to these developed recreation sites, the BLM offers four-wheel drive and off-road vehicle areas throughout the state, as well as numerous rock hounding sites. For rules, regulations and information on this form of Utah family recreation, contact BLM offices in Salt Lake City, Escalante, Monticello, Price, Moab, Hanksville, Fillmore, Vernal, Kanab or St. George. For addresses of these offices, see the appendix of this book.

Coyote

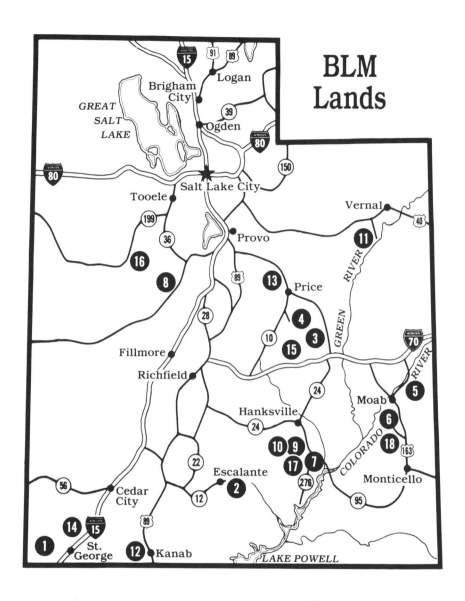

BLM Lands

1 BAKER RESERVOIR	**6** HATCH POINT
2 CALF CREEK	**7** HOG SPRINGS
3 CEDAR MOUNTAIN	**8** LITTLE SAHARA
4 DINOSAUR QUARRY	**9** LONESOME BEAVER
5 FISHER TOWERS	**10** McMILLAN SPRINGS

Buffaloberry

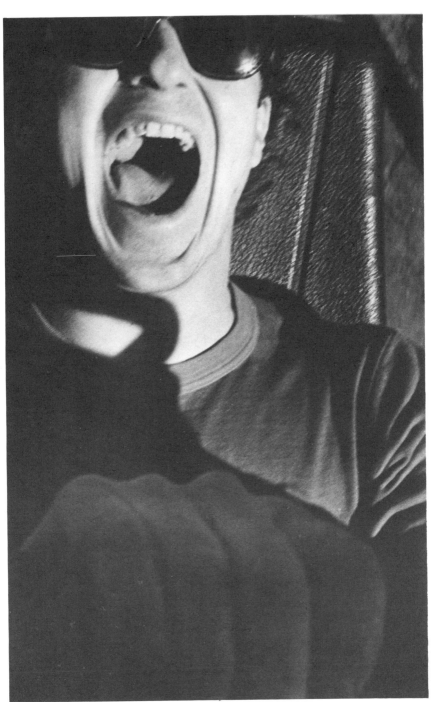

Lagoon Thrill Ride

CHAPTER SEVEN

Parks, Museums and Places of Interest

The young city dweller wandered about Wheeler Farm in a daze. He had heard about places like this in school but had never actually visited one himself.

There were chickens to feed, cows to milk and eggs to gather. Geese and ducks waddled through the yard, quacking and honking. There was an old house to explore, where women offered old-fashioned lemonade and bread made on a wood-burning stove. Children were taking a hayride in one field while a farmer was harvesting corn nearby. Pumpkins for Halloween grew in another field.

"So this is what things were like back in the olden days?" the child thought to himself. "That must have been a fun time to live."

Seeing the boy was fascinated, his parents studied a list of possible activities at Wheeler Farm. The farm, a historical area celebrating life at the turn of the century, is operated by the Salt Lake County Recreation, Parks and Multi-Purpose Center Division.

Mom and Dad discovered there was an annual Arbor Day tree planting, a day celebrating the adventures of Huck Finn, a pumpkin patch picnic, breakfasts on Pioneer Day and Labor Day, haunted woods during Halloween and a pioneer Christmas celebration.

With further study, they found there were rowboats and canoes for rent at a pond, a nature area along the banks of Little Cottonwood Creek, a daily chores' tour especially for children, and places for family reunions. There was storytime in Wheeler's Woods, a sledding hill for winter fun, and a fall festival. There were family garden classes, dutch oven cooking workshops, and varied educational programs for youngsters during the summer.

As the parents watched their child move from one activity to another, they were glad they had come.

There are a number of such family places throughout Utah. Some, like Wheeler Farm, are operated by local governments. Others, like amusement parks, doll museums and water slide parks, are owned by private concerns. Many areas are major tourist attractions while numerous others are small, out-of-the-way spots that might be overlooked.

Here is a glance at some of the family-oriented places that don't fit the categories of national parks or monuments, state parks or federally-managed trails and campgrounds. They include amusement parks, historical areas, museums, fish hatcheries, planetariums, major city parks, zoos and waterslides. They promise both to educate and amuse.

WHEELER FARM — Wheeler Farm is a living history museum located at 6351 South 900 East in Salt Lake County. A restored farm from the 1890 to 1918 pioneer era, it is listed on the National Register of Historic Places. Most of the activities here are free, though there are nominal charges for hayrides, storytime and classes. Picnic areas and covered meeting rooms are available year-round for family reunions. Children especially enjoy hands-on activities like the free chores tour at 4:30 p.m. (5:30 p.m. in the summer) where they get a chance to gather eggs and milk cows. For more information write to Wheeler Historic Farm, 6351 South 900 East, Salt Lake City, Utah 84121.

RONALD V. JENSEN LIVING HISTORICAL FARM — Located on Highway 89-91 six miles south of Logan, this inexpensive attraction is an outdoor museum program of Utah State University. It is a re-creation of a Mormon family farm in 1896. The farm includes 120 acres of fields, meadows, orchards and gardens and has a realistic selection of work horses, dairy cows, sheep, hogs and poultry. Each year, a number of hands-on farming activities like doing the laundry, sheep-shearing, carding and spinning wool, planting trees, threshing, ham curing and apple harvesting help children understand life during this era of Utah history. Children can play with toys like corn cob dolls, jump ropes, and barrel staves. Christmas programs include sleigh-rides on horse-drawn sleighs and talks on traditional pioneer holiday activities. Write to Ronald V. Jensen Historical Farm, Wellsville, Utah 84339 for information.

DAUGHTERS OF THE UTAH PIONEERS MUSEUM — Located on 300 North Main in Salt Lake City across from the State Capitol Building, this free museum celebrates Utah's pioneer heritage. One of the finest collections of pioneer memorabilia in the Intermountain West is on display. Paintings by noted Utah artists, an extensive doll collection, pianos, guns, quilts, flags, furniture, books, photographs and handmade shoes are exhibited. Kids especially like the doll collection and the old carriage house.

THE CHILDREN'S MUSEUM OF UTAH — This museum, located at 840 North 300 West in the old Wasatch Plunge Building, is one of the finest additions to family education and recreation in the Salt Lake area. At the museum, children are invited to pilot a 727 training jet, excavate the skeleton of a saber-toothed cat, work with computers, control a robot, create a petroglyph rubbing, implant an artificial heart, anchor a simulated news program on television, draw on an electronic blackboard or participate in a number of scientific experiments. The hands-on learning experiences are intended to encourage original thought and develop self-reliance and self-confidence. The museum sponsors a variety of events, workshops and lectures for children. For more information on its programs, write to The Children's Museum of Utah, 840 North 300 West, Salt Lake City, Utah 84103.

THE UTAH MUSEUM OF NATURAL HISTORY — Located on the University of Utah campus, this museum is one our children beg us to visit several times a year. Its Junior Science Academy program is a summer camping experience with field trips designed to inspire young scientists. The museum is open from 9:30 a.m. to 5:30 p.m. Monday through Saturday and noon to 5:00 p.m. Sunday. The museum's five permanent galleries feature exhibits on biology, minerals, geology, ecology and man. Displays of dinosaur bones and hands-on type exhibits are popular with children. Parents who take their time touring this museum can teach their children about natural history. Contact the museum's education department for information on current family field trips, lecture series, children's activities and the Junior Science Academy. Write to the University of Utah, Utah Museum of Natural History, Salt Lake City, Utah 84112 for information.

Hayride at Wheeler Farm

MUSEUM OF CHILDHOOD — This museum, located at 36 West Center in Provo, houses collections of antique toys, trains, trucks, stuffed bears, doll houses, miniatures, children's clothing, books, paper dolls and other items of interest and a children's book shop. It is open from 10:00 a.m. to 5:00 p.m. Tuesday through Saturday year-round and offers numerous activities.

HANSEN PLANETARIUM — Located at 15 South State Street in downtown Salt Lake City, Hansen Planetarium has introduced both adults and children to the wonderful world of the stars for many years. Star shows in the modern planetarium are an unusual form of entertainment for families, with new programs being added all the time. Families can see shows on topics ranging from new discoveries in space to science fiction. Programs designed specifically for children are featured on Saturdays and on weekday mornings during the summer. The annual children's festival each summer and the Star of Wonder show during the Christmas season are especially popular. One of the recent programs available for children at the Hansen Planetarium was Magic Under the Stars. It featured a children's star show, a puppet show, science sorcery and children's theater. A children's space library at the Planetarium is designed to introduce kids to the cosmos, black holes, robots and the edge of the universe. The library has a 1,000-volume collection and numerous space games. Call ahead for museum hours. Astronomy classes for children and families are available throughout the year as well as free star parties, where families are invited to observe the wonders of the universe through one of the largest telescopes available to the public in Utah. The parties are often held at an observatory at Stansbury Park. Laser-light shows and free lectures are geared toward families and nominal fees are charged for most shows. For current information on program times and special events, call 532-STAR for a recorded message or write to Hansen Planetarium, 15 South State Street, Salt Lake City, Utah 84111.

HOGLE ZOO — Located east of Salt Lake City at 2600 East Sunnyside Avenue, Hogle Zoo is open at 9:00 a.m. every day of the year, except Christmas and New Year's Day. The zoo closes at 4:30 p.m. in the winter and 6:00 p.m. in the summer. Admission fees are $3.00 for adults and $1.50 for children five through 16 and senior citizens. Youngsters four years and younger are admitted free. In addition to offering the best collection of animals in the Intermountain area, Hogle Zoo sponsors a variety of summer programs for children as well as a docent outreach program where zoo animals are taken into local schools. Classes give children a chance to closely examine zoo animals, learning about insects, zoo babies, reptiles and wildlife habitat. The 52-acre zoo has a children's petting zoo and a train ride. There are more than 1,000 animals for kids to see. For information write to Hogle Zoological Gardens, P.O. Box 8475, Salt Lake City, Utah 84108.

CRYSTAL HOT SPRINGS — Try taking the kids cross country skiing in nearby Logan Canyon and then dropping down for a middle-of-the-winter swim at this year-round resort located on Utah Highway 69 near Honeyville. Open 10:00 a.m. to 10:00 p.m. in the summer and noon to 10:00 p.m. in the winter, Crystal Springs has a freshwater swimming pool, hot mineral pools, sauna, steam room and water slide. Camping facilities are available.

Polar Bear at Hogle Zoo

Fun at Water Parks

WATER SLIDES — Many towns throughout Utah have parks and swimming areas featuring water slides. These slides usually consist of plastic tubes — fully or partly enclosed — with water running through them. Three of the largest are **Raging Waters**, located at 1200 West 1700 South in Salt Lake City; **Super Sliders** at the Point of the Mountain between Provo and Salt Lake City; and Ogden's **Wild Waters**. the smaller areas use a pay-by-the-ride program while the larger complexes cost between $6.00 and $9.00 for an all-day pass. Raging Waters, the largest water slide park in the state, has a one-half acre wild wave pool that creates its own waves, a Little Dipper pool for young children and an activity pool with shotgun slides, rope swings, diving rocks, lily pad walks and gang slides.

ALPINE SLIDE — This 3,000-foot long slide is located at the Park City ski resort. It is the summer version of bobsledding. Riders take the Pay Day chairlift to the top of the mountain where they pick up a specifically-designed sled to ride down the track. The riders control the speed of their sled. For information, write to Park City Ski Corporation, P.O. Box 39, Park City, Utah 84060.

LYTLE RANCH PRESERVE — This natural preserve is located in one of Utah's most unique areas, the Beaver Dam Wash. Over 180 species of birds have been sighted here. So have many other kinds of mammals. The ranch is owned by the Nature Conservancy and Brigham Young University. It is unique to Utah because it is an ecological transition zone on the edge of the Great Basin, Colorado Plateau and Mohave Desert Regions. There are things here that won't be found anywhere else in the state, including Gila Monsters and sidewinders. It is located 35 miles southwest of St. George off old Highway 91. For camping reservations, write to Preserve Manager, Lytle Ranch Preserve, P.O. Box 398, Santa Clara, Utah 84765.

Wild Wave Pool at Raging Waters

COLLEGE OF EASTERN UTAH PREHISTORIC MUSEUM —
Located in the Municipal Building just off Second East in Price, this small
museum is a convenient stop on the way to national or state parks in
southeastern Utah. The main attractions here are four dinosaur skeletons
from nearby Cleveland-Lloyd Dinosaur Quarry (see Bureau of Land
Management Chapter). These are authentic dinosaur bones (not the plaster
casts seen in many museums). There are fossils to learn about here, as well
as displays about the Fremont Indian village with a full-size teepee. Youth
lectures, movies and tours are offered. The museum is open from 9:00 a.m.
to 5:00 p.m. Monday through Saturday. For information, write to College
of Eastern Utah, Prehistoric Museum, Price, Utah 84501.

THE OGDEN NATURE CENTER — This relatively new facility,
located at 966 West 12th Street in Ogden, was established to reunite man
and nature for educational, scientific, cultural, recreational and spiritual
pursuits. Open 10:00 a.m. to 4:00 p.m. Monday through Saturday, visitors
discover a number of hands-on exhibits and self-guided nature trails. They
have an opportunity to view geese, deer, hawks and raccoons in a natural
setting. The center offers a number of "Super Saturday" programs for
children taught by local experts. A nature discovery program for four, five,
and six year olds is fun for young families. Sample subjects of children's
classes include "Sun Power," "Insects," "Role of Trees in Nature" and
"Geology." There is a small farm house and playground at the center. For
more information, write to Ogden Nature Center, 966 West 12th Street,
Ogden, Utah 84404.

Squirrel

EMERY COUNTY MUSEUM — Located in Castle Dale City Hall, this small museum contains displays of dinosaurs, ancient Indians, pioneers, cowboys and miners. Take your children to the pioneer-era classroom and the typical pioneer home. A re-created mercantile stocked with items used by early settlers, and the bones of a 22-foot Allosaurus dinosaur are among the exhibits. The museum is open 9:00 a.m. to 5:00 p.m. Monday through Friday and Saturdays from 1:00 to 5:00 p.m.

HELPER BICENTENNIAL MINING MUSEUM — This restored old hotel located at 294 South Main in Helper, will help answer questions about mining history. It has displays of mining and railroad tools and the old-world cultures brought to Carbon County by the pioneers who came to work in the mines. Children should look at a turn-of-the-century doctor's office and display of dental equipment. Both will make them thankful for modern technology. The museum is open Monday through Saturday, 10:00 a.m. to 3:00 p.m.

McCURDY HISTORICAL DOLL MUSEUM — This museum, located at 246 North 100 East in Provo, features a collection of more than 3,000 dolls with a new display every month. The museum is open in the winter Tuesday through Saturday from 1:00 to 5:00 p.m. and 10:00 a.m. to 6:00 p.m. in the summer. Programs on Saturdays often feature the McCurdy Story Princess telling stories relating to the displays and exhibits. These are often accompanied by a tea party. Displays include a parade of fashion, folk dress of the world, dramatic episodes in history, provincial dress of Spain, first ladies of America, women of the Bible, crusades and pilgrimages, rarely found boy dolls, American Indian dolls, wax dolls, scenes from pioneer America, antique dolls and storybook dolls. A movie on dolls and a museum shop add to the visit. Programs vary, but can include topics like "Black Is Beautiful," "Cabbage Patch Dolls" and "Christmas." For information on activities, write to McCurdy Historical Doll Museum, 246 North 100 East, Provo, Utah 84601.

JOHN HUTCHINGS MUSEUM OF NATURAL HISTORY — This small museum is located at 685 North Center Street in Lehi and is open weekdays from 9:00 a.m. to 4:00 p.m. Visitors can see a collection of Indian artifacts, pioneer and historical items, as well as natural history exhibits. The cost is $1.00 for adults and 50 cents for children.

BELMONT SPRINGS — This resort, located north of Tremonton and open April through September, has a swimming pool, hot tub, nine-hole golf course, campground and picnic facilities. Take I-15 north to Tremonton, then go 12 miles north on State Road 191 to Plymouth.

NORTH BOX ELDER COUNTY MUSEUM — Located in Tremonton, this small museum contains displays of pioneer artifacts with an emphasis on the Bear River Valley. It normally is open from 1:00 to 5:00 p.m. Monday through Friday.

Children's Garden at Liberty Park

LIBERTY PARK — There are many city parks throughout Utah to give families a break from long drives. This Salt Lake City park is one of the oldest and finest. A prominent attraction here is the **Tracy Aviary**. The eleven-acre living area for hundreds of birds includes the rare Andean condor and an excellent collection of waterfowl species. Admission is free. Of particular interest are bird shows offered on summer weekends. In addition to the aviary, Liberty Park has a modern children's play area much different than the average city park playground. My kids can spend hours here. The availability of canoe and paddleboat rentals, amusement park rides, tours of the old Chase House, a swimming pool and a large tennis complex make Liberty Park one of the state's most important family areas. It is located at 900 South 700 East in Salt Lake City.

CHERRY HILL — This used to be just a private campground. Now it features miniature golf, waterslides, aeroball, nightly entertainment, a batting range and two game areas open to campers and the general public. It is located north of Lagoon in Fruit Heights.

MILES GOODYEAR CABIN-PIONEER MUSEUM — Trapper Miles Goodyear visited the Ogden Valley years before the Mormon pioneers arrived, and his cabin, built in 1841, is believed to be the first permanent home constructed in Utah. It is located in Ogden next to Pioneer Hall Museum which houses a collection of pioneer photographs, artifacts and memorabilia. It is open June through September from 10:00 a.m. to 5:00 p.m.

Children's Garden at Liberty Park

UNION STATION — If your children like guns, trains and old cars, paying a visit to Ogden's Union Station might make a trip to the northern part of Utah worthwhile. The station, located in the center of Ogden, is the site of the famous Browning Arms Collection, a railroad museum and miniature model railroad. The Golden Spike Gem and Mineral Display, Browning-Kimball Classic Car Museum, Myra Powell Gallery and a gift shop are also here. It is open Monday through Saturday from 10:00 a.m. to 6:00 p.m. Children can take a ride on the Union Station Express, a miniature train that carries passengers to and from Union Station through Ogden's business and historic district.

49TH STREET GALLERIA — Located just off I-15 in Murray, this large indoor facility features miniature golf, bowling, roller skating, batting cages, food and dozens of games. It is open year-round. There is no entrance fee.

CACHE VALLEY CHEESE FACTORY — Perhaps it's because cheese is my favorite food, but when I'm near the tiny town of Amalga in Cache County, I always take the kids to the cheese factory where a free guided tour shows us how cheese is made. Like their father, the children enjoy the free samples. This isn't worth an all-day trip but is a nice spot to spend half an hour.

HEBER CREEPER STEAM TRAIN — Located in Heber City, the Heber Creeper is a turn-of-the-century steam train that makes two daily summer trips through lush Heber Valley and down Provo Canyon to Vivian Park near Bridal Veil Falls. Passengers enjoy the realistic train setting and a staged train robbery along the way. For information, write to Heber Creeper, P.O. Box 103, Heber, Utah 84032.

BRIDAL VEIL FALLS AND SKYTRAM — Located four miles east of Orem in Provo Canyon, the feathery falls cascade down the mountain into the Provo River. It's a thrill for kids to take a ride up the steepest skytram in the world. The tram is operated on a seasonal basis.

MONTE L. BEAN LIFE SCIENCE MUSEUM — This museum is located on the Brigham Young University campus in Provo. Exhibits and displays demonstrate the ecology of various natural habitats such as marshlands or beaver ponds. The museum has a large collection of trophy animals and shells as well. It is open daily, except Sunday. Entry is free.

SARATOGA RESORT — Saratoga Resort, located on the northwest corner of Utah Lake west of Lehi, is famous for its four natural warm-spring swimming pools. A large waterslide, go-kart track, boat harbor, arcade, picnic area, overnight campground and a few rides for younger children make it popular with families.

TRAFALGA FUN CENTER — Located just off I-15 near Orem, this facility features bumper boats, indoor and outdoor miniature golf, arcade games and a waterslide.

THE HOMESTEAD — Located in Midway, the Homestead is an old, southern-style hotel. Indoor and outdoor swimming pools, a naturally-heated hot tub, sauna, mineral pool and horseback rides are open to the public. Our family likes to take a winter ski trip to nearby Wasatch Mountain State Park and end the day with a warm swim in the hot springs pools.

HARDWARE RANCH — The ranch is located near the top of Blacksmith Fork Canyon near Hyrum in northern Utah. Many Utah families make a trek to Division of Wildlife Resources-operated Hardware Ranch each winter to enjoy a ride on the horse-drawn sled to view hundreds of elk wintering here. The visitor center features interpretive exhibits on the elk and other wildlife in the area. The trip up the canyon in the winter is scenic, with plenty of wildlife along the way.

Hardware Ranch

163

FISH HATCHERIES – The Division of Wildlife Resources operates a number of fish hatcheries throughout the state, including hatcheries like Midway, Kamas, Fountain Green, Springville, Mammoth Creek (near Bryce Canyon National Park), Mantua, Loa and Glenwood Springs in Sevier County. Perhaps the most interesting facility for children to visit is the Perry J. Egan hatchery south of Bicknell on the road to Capitol Reef National Park. This is where egg supplies for the state's other fish hatcheries come from, and there are many different varieties of large brood stock trout here to see. A tour of the facility will show how the eggs are stored and hatched. The hatchery is particularly interesting on days when biologists are stripping eggs from females and then fertilizing them by milking the males. We especially like the large, white albino rainbow trout which can easily be seen and photographed at the hatchery.

TEMPLE SQUARE – Whether you are a Mormon or not, one of the top family tourist destinations in Utah is Temple Square in the heart of Salt Lake City. Free half-hour tours are offered each day. Organ recitals in the famous Tabernacle are offered at noon Monday through Friday and at 4:00 p.m. on Saturday and Sunday. The Mormon Tabernacle Choir rehearses Thursday nights in the Tabernacle from 8:00 to 9:30 p.m. (come and go as you wish). Its Sunday morning broadcast is open to the public (be seated by 9:15 a.m.) and a Friday and Saturday evening (7:30 p.m.) concert series is also held in the Assembly Hall. The Genealogical Library and Museum of Church History and Art are nearby. My children like to visit Temple Square during the Christmas season, when a nativity scene and thousands of tiny lights turn Temple Square into a winter wonderland.

PARLEYS GULCH – Located near the mouth of Parleys Canyon at the eastern edge of Salt Lake City, this recently acquired city park is a nature preserve in the midst of an urban area. Take a morning or evening hike with children and point out wild birds and plants. Parley's Gulch is being developed as a nature center. Enter through Tanner Park.

LAGOON – Lagoon is located almost halfway between Ogden and Salt Lake just off I-15. It is the state's largest amusement park. Open weekends during the spring and fall and daily during the summer, Lagoon compares favorably with any amusement park in the United States. Its top ride attractions include an old-fashioned wooden roller coaster, a Colossal Fire Dragon roller coaster (featuring two upside down loops), and dozens of other rides. Musical productions, a wild West shootout, and the historical Pioneer Village museum add to the fun. Parents will appreciate the cleanliness of the park, its flower gardens and fountains. A large swimming pool, an opera house, summer concerts, rodeos, the Davis County Fair, many picnic areas and miniature golf make this a place where most Utah families spend at least one day a year. For the best bargain, purchase an unlimited ride pass.

Mormon Temple, Salt Lake City's Temple Square

Children's Skiing in Utah

CHAPTER EIGHT

Family Skiing

There was a time, when the children were five years old, that skiing was an exercise in frustration.

It would take hours to get them bundled up, into the car and on the slopes. The old, awkward cable bindings on their cross country equipment took a great deal of time to adjust. One pair always seemed to malfunction, sending the child into hysterics.

To adults accustomed to skiing for miles, the frustration continued once the skiing started. The kids were good for a few blocks and then became tired, scared or cold. Goals for a day of skiing were downscaled from miles to feet. If the children lasted an hour, it was considered a major accomplishment.

There were times when it seemed like the children would never learn to ski. On more than one occasion, the family returned home in tears, anger and frustration.

Through trial-and-error we finally found the right equipment and places to go. The children slowly grew out of their awkward phase and learned to ski. When they turned seven, it was possible to travel to Cedar Breaks National Monument in the winter and take an all-day tour. They begged us to take short trips to places like the Spruces in Big Cottonwood Canyon, where they could ski on a relatively flat track and crawl around and under the picnic tables now turned into snow caves by the snow. The once-frustrating trips up Millcreek Canyon turned into routine experiences. The children even asked for — and received — genuine three-pin ski outfits for Christmas. It wasn't long before they were searching for the tallest, longest hills to challenge their confidence and increasing skills.

We chose to teach our children cross country skiing first, though we love to downhill ski. Nordic skiing was initially less expensive and less threatening. This isn't to say we made the right choice. When at a resort, it is possible to see dozens of young children whizzing down the slopes. Kids like snow.

167

There are many family skiing oportunities in Utah. Many of the downhill resorts offer discounts to junior skiers. There are convenient places to rent or purchase both nordic and alpine ski equipment. Cross country and alpine ski programs for juniors are run by most resorts.

Keep in mind, children pick up skiing quickly and soon may be zooming past their parents. When selecting a resort in Utah, look for one that caters to the skills of your family; offers children's or family discounts; has a ski school; offers special rental-lesson packages; or has day care programs for children who aren't yet ready to ski.

Here is a look at some of Utah's ski areas for both downhill and cross country skiers, with an eye towards family winter fun:

Greatest Snow On Earth

Alta

Downhill Resorts

ALTA — One of the nation's oldest ski resorts, Alta has a reputation as a place where the experts ski. Yet, there are few better places for a child to learn than off the resort's 2.5-mile long Albion lift. While Alta does not offer children's discounts, it is less expensive to purchase a beginner's pass for its Albion, Cecret and Sunnyside lifts. The trails off these runs are heavily groomed every night. The lifts run slower as well.

Albion is a place to take youngsters who may own only cross country skis. A single lift ticket can be purchased at a nominal rate. A family can ski into the pretty Albion Basin campground for some flat-track skiing and a picnic before heading back down the trail along the road used by vehicles in the summer or on the beginner alpine run. The runs will be more challenging than a flat track experience, but kids looking for their first chance to ride a lift and who have experience on nordic skis should enjoy trying something like this.

More than one Utah skier has learned the basics by using one of the free rope tows at Alta that lead up to the lodges. Day care is available at the Albion Ticket Building for children six to 12 years of age.

Utah's Famous Powder Snow

BEAVER MOUNTAIN — Located in Logan Canyon, Beaver Mountain is a small, family-owned resort with beginner hills. It features discounted rates for children under 12 and senior citizens. The Little Beaver lift serves beginners. Gentle Ben, a two-mile run coming off Harry's Dream Lift, is a longer beginner's run.

BRIAN HEAD — Located east of Parowan, Brian Head is the largest ski area in southern Utah. It offers children's discounts, day care services and a kinderski program for children ages four to ten. The Riviera lift, which is separate from the expert runs, services three novice runs where children can get their ski legs before trying more difficult terrain. The 919-foot First Time run is a good place to start. A beginner lesson package including a two-hour lesson, rental equipment and a lift pass for the beginner hill is a bargain.

BRIGHTON — This Big Cottonwood Canyon resort east of Salt Lake City often bills itself as "The Place Utah Learns to Ski." Passes for the five lifts are among the most inexpensive in the United States. A child's discount pass is available. A learn-to-ski package which includes rental skis, a lift ticket and a lesson, is an inexpensive introduction to the sport. After a lesson, most beginners can ski on the Mary's or Majestic runs. We like to ski here at night, when the slopes are seldom crowded and we can practice our skiing without many folks watching us.

DEER VALLEY — This is the newest addition to the Park City ski scene and the state's most exclusive — and expensive — resort. There are some amenities here that families with some extra money will appreciate. The Burns Lift services a beginner hill separate from the rest of the resort. A training chair operating like a tiny carousel teaches kids how to get on a lift. The grooming here is superb and discounts for children and senior citizens are available.

ELK MEADOWS/MT. HOLLY — This growing resort is located in southern Utah's Beaver County. About 40 percent of the runs are rated as "beginner." Children's discounts are available.

NORDIC VALLEY — This small resort is located east of Ogden. It is open during the daytime only on weekends but prides itself on its night skiing. Children's discount prices and a well-established ski racing program are available.

PARK CITY — Utah's largest ski resort, Park City offers a number of programs for families. The First Time and Three Kings lifts serve novice runs. Skiing off the Gondola is convenient for families who have skiers of different ability levels. The runs end in the same place, but there are hills for experts, intermediates and beginners. The beginner run is 3.5-miles long. A discount is available for children under the age of 12 and senior citizens (those over 70) ski free. There is a Kinderschule ski program including lunch and lessons for kids three to six years in age. The resort has a day care center.

PARKWEST — With two beginner lifts and hills, this is where I learned to ski. Many junior high and high schools take advantage of lessons offered here. The resort has some steep slopes for families with better skiers. A family discount pass, children's discount ticket and less expensive rates for the two beginner lifts are available. A Kinderschule beginner program for three-year-olds is offered.

POWDER MOUNTAIN — East of Ogden, this resort has three lifts serving three mountains. The night skiing hill is best for beginners, though it may be a little difficult for first-timers. Children's discount passes are available.

SNOWBASIN — Ogden's largest ski resort has two novice lifts, Becker and Little Cat, discount passes for children six to 12 and for the Becker and Little Cat lifts.

SNOWBIRD — Located in Little Cottonwood Canyon east of Salt Lake City, Snowbird is a modern full-service resort with a reputation as an expert ski area. Yet, it has classes for children, day care facilities for children of lodge guests and children's and senior citizen's passes. The small Chickadee lift near the condominiums is short and easy and allows parents to watch their kids ski.

SOLITUDE — Located just below Brighton in Big Cottonwood Canyon, Solitude has recently undergone a major expansion program. It is an inexpensive ski area for families on a budget. Its Sesame Street Run is easy and usually uncrowded. The resort's Skiwee all-day program is for novice skiers and includes a hot lunch. Solitude, however, is best for skiers with a little more experience.

Cross Country Skiing at Brighton

SUNDANCE — Actor Robert Redford's Provo Canyon resort offers a big discount for children. It does not have as many beginner runs as some of the other resorts, but has some quality night skiing. Sundance's beginner-to-intermediate terrain lends itself to families with some skiing experience.

Cross Country Skiing

The **White Pine Ski Touring Center** in Park City, the **Brighton Ski Touring Center** at the top of Big Cottonwood Canyon and **Wasatch Mountain State Park** offer rentals, groomed track skiing and lessons for cross country skiers. For novices, skiing a groomed track is a definite advantage.

Families with a sense of adventure might enjoy an overnight, guided Yurt Tour from the Brighton Touring Center. A yurt is a circular domed tent. The Brighton Touring Center version is situated high in the Wasatch Mountains and outfitted with a wood burning stove for heat, a propane stove for cooking, kitchen utensils and bunk beds for eight people.

Cross country skiers can rent winterized cabins at **Camp Roger**, located in the **Soapstone Basin** near the High Uintas Wilderness Area. Reservations must be made at the Salt Lake branch of the YMCA.

Many of the state's golf courses turn into cross country ski areas in the winter with informal tracks laid down after each snow. Mountain Dell Golf Course, located in Parleys Canyon just east of Salt Lake City, is a particular favorite for young families just learning to ski. Its clubhouse is often open during the winter months, providing a place for young children to warm themselves on cold days. Wasatch Mountain State Park, located near Midway, has good track skiing. There is a small charge. Families may enjoy a nordic ski tour at Wasatch Mountain and then a winter dip in the indoor and outdoor natural hot springs pools at the privately-operated Homestead Resort a short drive from the park.

Nearly every U.S. Forest Service Canyon in the state — and there are dozens — is a possible family cross country ski area. There is a potential for conflicts with snowmobiles in a few of the mountain areas, so check with the state Division of Parks and Recreation for Utah's snowmobile complexes. The Utah Department of Highways closes some roads in the winter — the roads in Millcreek and East Canyons east of Salt Lake City are examples. The closed roads become easy nordic ski areas. There are dozens of small ski trails marked by the U.S. Forest Service around the state. The Beaver Creek Trailhead east of Kamas, the Spruces in Big Cottonwood Canyon and a trail in Logan Canyon are excellent family ski areas. Check with the local ranger district of the U.S. Forest Service for trail information.

Cross Country Skiing

Hiking With Small Children

CHAPTER NINE

Putting It All Together

There are some things about a vacation that simply aren't much fun. Long, hot drives with screaming children in the back seat; crowded, noisy campgrounds; disappointing attractions; overpacked cars; and unexpected expenses can all ruin a family travel experience.

While things will sometimes go wrong despite the best laid plans, taking the time to plan a family vacation can often be as enjoyable as taking the vacation itself. Let your children be a part of the process. Ask them where they would like to go, show them how to plan a vacation budget and teach them how to read a road map while you drive. Acquaint them with the state by telling them the names of county seats and local mountain ranges. The chapters in this book were designed to help Utah families learn where they can enjoy a vacation with their children in their home state, as well as to introduce newcomers to the Beehive State's many recreation areas. The appendix at the back of this book suggests some places where more detailed information can be obtained. Yet, it is important to decide exactly what kind of a vacation you want for your family. Utah families should ask themselves some questions before planning a trip close to home.

Is your family going out for the weekend, or will this be an extended vacation?

Are you interested in concentrating on one small area? If so, are you looking for a particular type of experience? For example, do you want to go fishing or hiking?

Are you going to stay in a motel or lodge, or will you camp?

What are the capabilities of your children? Can they hike a few blocks, a mile or a long distance?

What interests your children? What interests you? Does your family like dinosaurs, Indians, trains, living history exhibits, amusement parks, nature trails, campfire programs, boating, swimming or museums?

How important is solitude? Are you willing to sacrifice some comfort or drive farther to avoid the big crowds at major attractions?

Do you want your vacation to be an educational experience? Answering these questions can help you make the most of your leisure time. But how can you put together the kind of trip you want in a limited amount of time while on a tight budget?

Any person could spend a lifetime traveling and still never see all of Utah. Researching this book has opened up a number of new places for my family to explore, and we've spent years trying to see every part of our home state.

Despite the various differences between families, some assumptions can be made about the major attractions people will want to see in Utah. Tops on nearly everyone's list are usually the five national parks — Arches, Bryce Canyon, Capitol Reef, Canyonlands and Zion — as well as the Great Salt Lake and the Salt Lake Mormon Temple. A family can get a glimpse of these major attractions in a week-long trip through the state.

Every family is different. What we like to do is pick a home base for a weekend, four-day or one-week vacation and then proceed to see the sights from this spot. We don't like to set up camp, break it down and then set it up again night after night unless we absolutely have to. If we want solitude, we pick a less well-known area to camp and then travel to the more popular spots. If we are in the mood for campfire programs and interpretive activities, we camp at a more developed site. Or, if we choose not to rough it, we stay at a motel or a lodge.

The following suggestions will be useful in helping you organize and plan a trip:

Take, for example, a trip to **Zion National Park**. A quick look at a state road map will show you that, within a two-hour drive of Zion National Park, a family could visit any one of the following: Cedar Breaks National Monument, Bryce Canyon National Park, Pipe Spring National Monument, Navajo and Panguitch Lakes in the Dixie National Forest, Snow Canyon and Coral Pink Sand Dunes State Parks, the Bureau of Land Management's Dixie National Forest, St. George and Cedar City.

The same methods for planning a trip can be used when seeing other areas around the state. Here are some possible combinations with major attractions listed as the home bases:

BRYCE CANYON NATIONAL PARK: Bryce Canyon is surrounded by the Dixie National Forest and a great deal of Bureau of Land Management public property. Side trips can be made to Kodachrome Basin State Park, Escalante Petrified Forest State Park and Anasazi Indian Village State Park along State Highway 12. If a dirt road doesn't deter you, the trip between Kodachrome Basin and U.S. 89 is fascinating, with Grosvenor Arch and Cottonwood Canyon the highlights. The road comes out near Glen Canyon Dam and Lake Powell, but can be in poor condition. The BLM's Calf Creek Campground and Calf Creek Falls nature trail are nearby. The U.S. Forest Service's Red Canyon on the way to Bryce Canyon

Hiking With Kids Can Be Challenging

National Park has a campground and nature trail. The BLM's Devil's Garden scenic area is just south of Escalante. Pipe Spring National Monument and Cedar Breaks National Monument, Zion National Park and Coral Pink Sand Dunes State Park are all located in the surrounding area.

CAPITOL REEF NATIONAL PARK: The Boulder Mountain area on U.S. Forest Service land is adjacent to Capitol Reef and is a cooler camping and fishing area during the hot summer. Fish Lake has lodge facilities and campgrounds suitable for families. The Perry Egan Fish Hatchery near Bicknell is worth an hour's stop to allow your kids to see dozens of large fish. Goblin Valley State Park is a short drive east to Hanksville and then north. Lake Powell's Hite Marina as well as Natural Bridges National Monument are in the vicinity on State Highway 95.

ARCHES NATIONAL PARK: Dead Horse Point State Park and the newly paved Island in the Sky District of Canyonlands National Park are both located a short drive from Arches. Fisher Towers up the Colorado River from Moab is a popular scenic attraction. The Manti LaSal National Forest offers families a forested loop drive, some fishing at Ken's Lake and a place to cool off from the desert. The drive to the Needles District of Canyonlands National Park or BLM campgrounds at Hatch Point and Windwhistle isn't a long one. The town of Moab, located on the outskirts of Arches National Park, has three private campgrounds with swimming pools. Lodging and a number of family-oriented activities such as river-running, horseback and four-wheeler trips are available here. Older kids might enjoy renting mountain bikes or BMX bicycles and riding on the slickrock trail on BLM land just outside of town.

CANYONLANDS NATIONAL PARK: The Squaw Flat campground in the Needles District, though 35 miles from the nearest major highway (U.S. 163) could be a base for several days of vacation. So could the three U.S. Forest Service campgrounds in the nearby Manti-LaSal National Forest west of Monticello. Things to see in this area include Hovenweep and Natural Bridges National Monuments (both have campgrounds), Edge of the Cedars State Park in Blanding, Newspaper Rock State Park and the Goosenecks of the San Juan State Park.

THE WASATCH FRONT: The area classified as the Wasatch Front begins in Nephi and goes north to the Idaho state line. There are dozens of campgrounds, cultural sights, ski areas, historical areas, amusement parks, water slides, fishing spots and state parks along the Front. Using Salt Lake City as a base, you can visit the Great Salt Lake, Mormon Temple, Hogle Zoo, Lagoon Amusement Park, ski resorts in Park City, Cottonwood Canyons and any number of museums and historical areas. Campgrounds and forest picnic areas can be found in the Wasatch Mountains east of all the major cities. Major reservoirs like Deer Creek, Rockport, Echo, East Canyon, Pine View, Willard Bay and Hyrum provide water recreation. For residents, many of these close-to-home areas make relaxing weekend trips.

Desert Hiking

FLAMING GORGE NATIONAL RECREATION AREA: There are dozens of U.S. Forest Service campgrounds around Flaming Gorge Reservoir. Red Fleet, Steinaker and Starvation Reservoirs also offer campgrounds and water-oriented sports. With raft rentals available, a float trip down the Green River below the Flaming Gorge Dam is a possible family outing. There is a state natural history museum in Vernal with dinosaur gardens young children like. The Dinosaur National Monument is nearby.

Utah Theme Trips

While these regional areas offer some family recreation experiences, our family has often planned an entire summer around a particular educational theme.

For example, my kids are fascinated by dinosaurs. We've spent a summer taking trips to various areas where dinosaurs can be studied. For example, even before leaving Salt Lake City, we visited the Utah Museum of Natural History on the University of Utah campus to introduce the kids to dinosaur skeletons. Then, we started taking short excursions away from home. We spent a weekend seeing the Utah Fieldhouse of Natural History Museum in Vernal with its dinosaur garden and nearby Dinosaur National Monument. Here the kids could see bones being excavated from a dinosaur quarry. We took another trip to the small museum in Price and the Cleveland-Lloyd Dinosaur Museum in Emery County. By the end of the summer, our children regarded themselves as dinosaur experts.

A family could spend a summer studying Utah pioneer history. Visit the Old Deseret village at Pioneer Trails State Park, the Daughters of the

Fishing at Crouse Reservoir

182

Kids Fishing

Utah Pioneers Museum and Wheeler Farm on short trips in Salt Lake City. Spend some time at Lagoon's Pioneer Village. Take a day trip to the Union Station and Fort Buenventura State Park in Ogden. Or, spend a day seeing a special activity at the Ronald Jensen Historical Farm in Logan. Go over to Camp Floyd and the Stagecoach Inn State Parks in Tooele County. Learn about the mining boom by visiting the small museum at Helper. Visit a living history exhibit at Pipe Spring National Monument on the Utah-Arizona border. If you take these trips before or shortly after your children study Utah history in school, the things they learn will be more meaningful to them.

Other "theme" possibilities include Utah wildlife, the study of local Indian cultures, following the paths of the Pony Express or the Dominguez-Escalante Trails, bird identification at Utah bird refuges or Utah geology. Organizations like Canyonlands Field Institute, Utah Museum of Natural History, Hogle Zoo and Hansen Planetarium offer family field trips that fit into these themes.

One final piece of advice. Don't be reluctant to use government agencies to get help. The National Park Service, Divisions of Parks and Recreation and Wildlife Resources, the Utah Travel Council, U.S. Forest Service, Bureau of Land Management and dozens of local chambers of commerce are more than willing to answer your questions or provide you with dozens of free brochures, maps and lodging information. Addresses of some of these sources are listed in the appendix.

Wilderness Solitude

CHAPTER TEN

Teaching Children Outdoor Ethics

My ten-year-old daughter examined the fly fishing vest closely, sticking her fingers in every pocket and unzipping every zipper. Looking like a detective in search of a clue, she examined knives, boxes of flies, old bottles of rotten salmon eggs and rusted hooks.

Emma had not fished a stream before and now on a clear July morning we stood on a small tributary of Strawberry Reservoir in the Uinta National Forest. Dozens of small streams, closed to fishing early in the season to protect the spawning run of hundreds of native cutthroat trout, had opened the day before.

As we approached the first deep pool on the tiny stream, I offered my daughter some wisdom that had been passed on to me over the years by other stream fishermen.

"Be quiet," I told her. "You have to creep up on a hole and dangle your hook over the side. Try not to let the fish see your shadow. If it does, it will get spooked and hide under a bank. We might not see it again."

Emma was fascinated by the process. The stream was clear, and she could watch small trout, suckers and chubs dart in and out of the reeds and underbrush of the stream.

The Strawberry Valley, long a favorite of mine, had never been greener. The wildflowers surrounded us in shades of yellow, white and purple. The scene was idyllic, except for the pop cans and candy wrappers left by fishermen who had lined the banks of these streams the day before.

That's where the smelly old creel on my fly fishing vest came in handy.

As a fly fisherman, my skills lie somewhere between beginner and novice. I'm more apt to catch a tree branch, the back of my neck, or a nearby fence than I am a trout. But, part of the fun of being a fly fisherman is picturing yourself a purist. I rationalized that—because I was going to release any trout I caught no matter what—I might as well use the creel on my fishing vest for something. I found it worked just fine as a place to put old pop cans, candy wrappers and other unsightly trash.

Getting a limit of pop cans is never difficult. There always seems to be litter in the outdoors. Trying to teach Emma that one does not always have to keep fish to have fun (though it would be nice to catch one once in awhile), we found that filling the creel with litter was much easier than filling it with trout. Before long, it was full.

It would have been easy to have allowed this litter to upset us, but there was something satisfying about clearing the meadow of trash especially with my daughter there to learn the lesson I was trying to teach. Besides, I reasoned, perhaps the "fish gods" would smile on me if I picked up after people who had been here before.

Obviously, there are no such things as "fish gods." But there were killdeer in the neighborhood, who nervously watched me get too close to their nests. We caught a fleeting glimpse of a baby duck before it quickly waddled to the safety of nearby brush.

Emma and I began studying the small fish in the stream, trying to learn their habits. We watched the movements of the fish, discovering much about their aquatic environment in the process. We looked for the type of insects they were eating, at how the fish approached their prey and whether the fish were facing upstream or down.

Children and adults learn much from one another in this kind of environment, even though lectures are often transparent. A lack of knowledge in such situations is fatal because a child will immediately ask a difficult question or put a parent in an embarrassing situation.

Take, for example, lectures on ethics.

These little talks are usually reserved for special times in special places. Father suddenly becomes the perfect parent, who would enforce every rule and would never dream of allowing an outdoor injustice.

There was the time we visited a tide pool on the Pacific Ocean. Having never seen such a thing, my children were entranced.

The tide was out and many of the small creatures trapped in the pool around the rocky reef became interesting objects of study. A teacher from a nearby school watched the kids racing about and offered to give them a brief ecology lesson.

She showed them how a small tuft of what looked like grass was really a living sea creature. When it was touched, it squirted water. She showed them where to look for a starfish and found a jellyfish for them to examine.

The kids were amazed. They listened to her every word as if it were the gospel. This, obviously, was a special person in a special place. Her words were not to be ignored.

"Study these things and enjoy them," she told the children. "But leave them here. A starfish that looks so beautiful on the beach will just gather dust on the shelf at home."

One is never certain how children take such advice. On this cold, windy morning, with the smell of the sea breeze and a feeling of wildness in the air, the kids' senses came alive. They danced from rock to rock, singing songs of the sea and looking for new and exciting creatures. Their imaginations ran wild.

Emma has always had a reputation in the family as "The Enforcer." It is well earned. She has a strong sense of right and wrong, and she'll argue her case with friends, adults, parents and, most especially, younger brothers. We fancy her growing up to be a wealthy lawyer.

Emma saw some kids seize a starfish out of the tide pool and stuff it into a plastic bag. Pleased with their trophy, they began walking quickly toward their parents in a waiting car.

My daughter began to sob.

"Daddy," she wailed, "they can't take that starfish away from its home! They're going to kill it! Don't let them take it!"

Now what? On one hand, my daughter was sobbing and looking for her father to save the day. On the other hand, the father of those children may have been six-foot-seven and a pro wrestler who happened to see nothing wrong with collecting starfish.

There was only one thing to do. I sent my wife to solve the problem.

Northern Leopard Frog

She tried to talk some sense into the children. But it was no use. Those kids ignored her and laughed as they ran away with their trophy.

Emma and her brothers were crushed. So were we. Lessons are difficult to understand when the object of that lesson is suddenly destroyed. Besides, how would you like to have a wimp for a father?

It was like that a few years ago on a Labor Day backpacking trip to Utah's High Uintas Wilderness Area.

The kids were veterans of many car camping trips, but had never before stayed in the woods far away from civilization (at least a mile). We found a little lake after a short walk, and it was time to make camp. The children were excited to have the place to themselves.

They played in the meadow and scrambled on rocks. Advised not to pick the wildflowers so they could be enjoyed by any visitor who chanced along, the children made friends with all of nature. They danced and sang in the meadow. Even our youngest son, Bryer, still in diapers, caught the spirit of things as he rolled in the grass.

We had walked only a half mile off the road. With the nearby car-camping areas jammed with hundreds of Labor Day weekend visitors, that had made all the difference. Only one other party was camped on the lake, and it was almost out of sight.

There were chances for teaching ethical lessons everywhere and, being ever the outdoor purist, I didn't ignore any of them.

The kids wondered why we didn't build a fire, and we explained about how a firepit would leave a black scar on the pristine meadow. They wondered why we couldn't bury the little one's soiled diapers, no doubt wishing they wouldn't have to carry them out. We explained that they would soon come back to the surface and never disintegrate.

"Always leave a camp in better condition than you found it," I said, repeating an old saying my father had taught me.

The next morning, as we wandered to a different meadow, the unmistakable sound of an engine could be heard breaking the silence of the morning. A four-wheel-drive vehicle was headed toward our meadow.

By the time we reached the meadow, the vehicle was gone. But it had left its mark. Right through the middle of what had been a virgin flower garden, were tire tracks in the mud: tracks that had crushed the wildflowers we had been so considerate not to pick the day before.

Angry, we tried to follow the tracks to see if we could find the culprits who had, for their own selfish reasons, violated our meadow. The four-wheelers had disappeared.

Some lessons are easier to learn.

Once, we took a walk with a National Park Service Ranger at Chaco Canyon National Monument in New Mexico. Because it is so remote, this monument gets limited visitation.

We had a ranger to ourselves, and she painted a wonderful picture of

Horseback Riding

Indian life hundreds of years before, showing us different parts of the Anasazi ruins.

As we walked through the crumbled remains of Pueblo Bonito, one of my children bent down to pick up a piece of broken pottery. Because Chaco Canyon was a place where such pottery was in wide use by the ancient Indians, it was easy to find such broken pieces.

"Please leave that where you found it," the ranger said in a gentle, but firm, voice. "There might be other pieces of pottery around. Perhaps, just perhaps, a scientist will come along some day and need that piece to solve a puzzle."

The ranger explained that archaeologists sometimes find different pieces of pottery at different levels of diggings. Finding a certain piece in a particular location could supply important information and help solve an ancient puzzle.

Impressed and a little chagrined, the child carefully put the piece back where he found it. The rest of the trip, the kids viewed pottery pieces as something to study with their eyes. Because of the ranger's words, they never again removed something from a national park, preferring to "leave only footprints and take only pictures." Lessons on outdoor ethics can be difficult to learn. They can also be painful to parents who are usually less than perfect. There is something unnerving about giving your child a lecture on the evils of littering and then being caught inadvertently leaving a gum wrapper on top of a picnic table.

Which brings us back to that day on the stream.

Two young cutthroat trout faced upstream in a ripple and Emma and I studied them with great interest. I slipped my spinner into the water just above them and jigged it gently. Suddenly, much to my surprise, one of the fish hit it and was hooked. I reeled him in as quickly as I could and, because he was so small, he didn't put up much of a fight.

Thankful I was using a spinner instead of bait, I easily slipped the hook out of the trout's lip and released it back to the stream, making certain that Emma saw the proper way to release a fish unharmed. I hope I taught her correctly. I don't often catch a trout on a stream.

In any case, my daughter, the fish and I were all wiser.

We kept walking down the stream, trying to perfect our fishing technique. One trout, perhaps ten inches long, gave me a start by acting like it might take the lure. It suddenly turned away, no doubt startled by Emma's delighted scream. Another four-incher was finally hooked and quickly released.

It was time to leave. My daughter had tired of her father's lectures and my wife and youngest child were hot and thirsty.

There I was, left with a creel full of pop cans, an unfulfilled dream of catching a trophy cutthroat and my memories. One doesn't always have to catch his limit to have fun. Unless, of course, it's a limit of pop cans he's after.

Square Tower Ruin at Hovenweep National Monument

A Tiny Goblin at Goblin Valley State Park

APPENDIX

Where to Get More Information

There are a number of places where a family can find out more about places they are interested in visiting. Government agencies, private publishers and private museum and campground operators are more than willing to furnish free information on request. Detailed guide books have been written on many of the subjects which have been covered in this book.

Here is a list of places where a family traveler can obtain information when on the road or when simply planning a vacation:

UTAH TRAVEL COUNCIL
Council Hall/Capitol Hill
Salt Lake City, Utah 84114
Phone: 533-5681
Recorded summer calendar of events and winter snow conditions, call 521-8102
*Provides multi-purpose maps, travel publications, posters

U.S. GEOLOGICAL SURVEY
125 South State
Salt Lake City, Utah 84138
Phone: 524-5652
*Topographical and geological maps, publications

AERONAUTICAL OPERATIONS DIVISION
135 North 2400 West
Salt Lake City, Utah 84116
Phone: 533-5057
*Airport directory
*Aeronautical charts, regulations

UTAH CAMPGROUND OWNERS ASSOCIATION VIP CAMPGROUND
1370 West North Temple
Salt Lake City, Utah 84116
Phone: 521-2682
*Information on private campgrounds within Utah

UTAH DIVISION OF WILDLIFE RESOURCES
1596 West North Temple
Salt Lake City, Utah 84116
Phone: 533-9333
Recorded Information:
Hunting: 530-1297, Fishing: 530-1298, Birds: 530-1299
*Hunting and fishing information
*Bird refuges

UTAH ARTS COUNCIL
617 East South Temple
Salt Lake City, Utah 84102
Phone: 533-5895
*General information and publications pertaining to Utah arts organizations
*Utah Arts Resources Directory
*Glendenning Gallery and Chase Home Exhibition, featuring the State Fine Arts
  Collection

UTAH DEPARTMENT OF PUBLIC SAFETY
4501 South 2700 West
Salt Lake City, Utah 84119
Phone 965-4461 for administration; 965-4518 for Utah Highway Patrol

UTAH DEPARTMENT OF TRANSPORTATION
4501 South 2700 West
Salt Lake City, Utah 84119
Road Report Message: 964-6000 (Salt Lake Area) or 1-800-752-7600
  (toll free anywhere within Utah)
*Utah Highway Map
*Road conditions, construction sites

UTAH GEOLOGICAL AND MINERAL SURVEY
606 Black Hawk Way
Salt Lake City, Utah 84108
Phone: 581-6831
*Numerous publications on all aspects of Utah geology
*Resource library

UTAH GUIDES AND OUTFITTERS
Box 21242
Salt Lake City, Utah 84121
Phone: 943-6707
*Directory of professional river runners, outfitters

UTAH HERITAGE FOUNDATION
355 Quince Street
Salt Lake City, Utah 84103
Phone: 533-0858
*Private non-profit organization
*Historic Salt Lake City tours
*Publications

UTAH HOTEL/MOTEL ASSOCATION
9 Exchange Place, Suite 715
Salt Lake City, Utah 84111
Phone: 359-0104
*Information on accommodations

UTAH SKI ASSOCIATION
307 West 200 South
Suite 5005
Salt Lake City, Utah 84101
Phone: 534-1779
*Utah Ski Planner

UTAH STATE HISTORICAL SOCIETY
300 Rio Grande
Salt Lake City, Utah 84101
Phone: 533-5755
*Library: Utah, Mormons, the West
*Photograph collection: Utah, Mormons
*Historical publications
*Historic preservation

U.S. Forest Service Offices

INTERMOUNTAIN REGION HEADQUARTERS
U.S. Forest Service
324 25th Street
Ogden, Utah 84401
Phone: 625-5182

ASHLEY NATIONAL FOREST

Ashley National Forest
Headquarters
Ashton Energy Center
1680 West Highway 40, Suite 1150
Vernal, Utah 84078
Phone: 789-1181

Flaming Gorge Ranger District
Headquarters
P.O. Box 278
Manila, Utah 84046
Phone: 784-5445

Flaming Gorge Ranger District
Dutch John Office
P.O. Box 157
Dutch John, Utah 84023
Phone: 885-3338

Vernal Ranger District
650 North Vernal Avenue
Vernal, Utah 84078
Phone: 789-0323

Roosevelt Ranger District
West Highway 40
P.O. Box 338
Roosevelt, Utah 84066
Phone: 722-5018

Duchesne Ranger District
85 West Main
P.O. Box 1
Duchesne, Utah 84021
Phone: 738-2482

DIXIE NATIONAL FOREST

Dixie National Forest
Headquarters
82 North 100 East
P.O. Box 580
Cedar City, Utah 84720
Phone: 586-2421

Pine Valley Ranger District
196 East Tabernacle Street
P.O. Box 584
St. George, Utah 84770
Phone: 673-3431

Cedar City Ranger District
82 North 100 East
P.O. Box 627
Cedar City, Utah 84720
Phone: 586-4462

Powell Ranger District
225 East Center
P.O. Box 80
Panguitch, Utah 84759
Phone: 676-8815

Escalante Ranger District
270 West Main
P.O. Box 246
Escalante, Utah 84726
Phone: 826-4221

Teasdale Ranger District
P.O. Box 99
Teasdale, Utah 84773
Phone: 425-3435

FISHLAKE NATIONAL FOREST

Fishlake National Forest
Headquarters
115 East 900 North
Richfield, Utah 84701
Phone: 896-4491

Fillmore Ranger District
390 South Main
P.O. Box 265
Fillmore, Utah 84631
Phone: 743-5721

Loa Ranger District
150 South Main
P.O. Box 128
Loa, Utah 84747
Phone: 836-2811

Beaver Ranger District
190 North 100 East
P.O. Box E
Beaver, Utah 84713
Phone: 438-2436

Richfield Ranger District
115 East 900 North
Richfield, Utah 84701
Phone: 896-4491

MANTI-LASAL NATIONAL FOREST

Manti-LaSal National Forest
Headquarters
599 West Price River Drive
Price, Utah 84501
Phone: 637-2817

Moab Ranger District
446 South Main Street
Moab, Utah 84532
Phone: 259-7155

Monticello Ranger District
185 North 1st East
P.O. Box 820
Monticello, Utah 84535
Phone: 587-2114

Sanpete Ranger District
150 South Main Street
P.O. Box 692
Ephraim, Utah 84627
Phone: 283-4151

Ferron Ranger District
98 South State
P.O. Box 310
Ferron, Utah 84523
Phone: 384-2372

Price Ranger District
10 North Carbon Avenue
Price, Utah 84501
Phone: 637-2817

UINTA NATIONAL FOREST

Uinta National Forest
Headquarters
88 West 100 North
P.O. Box 1428
Provo, Utah 84603
Phone: 377-5780

Heber Ranger District
125 East 100 North
P.O. Box 190
Heber City, Utah 84032
Phone: 654-0470

Pleasant Grove Ranger District
390 North 100 East
P.O. Box 228
Pleasant Grove, Utah 84062
Phone: 785-3563

Spanish Fork Ranger District
44 West 400 North
Spanish Fork, Utah 84660
Phone: 798-3571

WASATCH-CACHE NATIONAL FOREST

Wasatch-Cache National Forest
Headquarters
8226 Federal Building
125 South Street
Salt Lake City, Utah 84138
Phone: 524-5030

Salt Lake Ranger District
6944 South 3000 East
Salt Lake City, Utah 84121
Phone: 524-5042

Kamas Ranger District
50 East Center Street
P.O. Box 68
Kamas, Utah 84036
Phone: 783-4338

Evanston Ranger District
103 Highway 150 South
Suite A
P.O. Box FS
Evanston, Wyoming 82930
Phone: 789-3194 — Winter
Phone: 642-6662 — Summer

Mountain View Ranger District
Lone Tree Road, Highway 44
P.O. Box 129
Mountain View, Wyoming 82939
Phone: 782-6555

Ogden Ranger District
Federal Building, Room 2005
324 25th Street
P.O. Box 1433
Ogden, Utah 84402
Phone: 625-5112

Logan Ranger District
910 South
Highway 89-91
Logan, Utah 84321
Phone: 753-2772

Bureau of Land Management Offices

Utah State Office
394 South State Street, Suite 301
Coordinated Financial Services Building
Salt Lake City, Utah 84111-2303

Salt Lake District Office
Bear River Resource Area
Pony Express Resource Area
2370 South 2300 West
Salt Lake City, Utah 84119
Phone: 524-5348

Cedar City District Office
176 East D.L. Sargent Drive
P.O. Box 724
Cedar City, Utah 84720
Phone: 586-2401

Dixie Resource Area
225 North Bluff
P.O. Box 726
St. George, Utah 84770
Phone: 673-4654

Kanab Resource Area
320 North First East
P.O. Box 458
Kanab, Utah 84741
Phone: 644-2672

Escalante Resource Area
Escalante, Utah 84726
Phone: 826-4291

Richfield District Office
150 East 900 North
Richfield, Utah
Phone: 896-8221

Warm Springs Resource Area
P.O. Box 778
Fillmore, Utah 84631
Phone: 743-6811

Sevier River Resource Area
180 North 100 East
P.O. Box 705
Richfield, Utah 84701
Phone: 896-8228

San Juan Resource Area
435 North Main Street
P.O. Box 7
Monticello, Utah 84535
Phone: 587-2141

Vernal District Office
Diamond Mountain Resource Area
Book Cliffs Resource Area
170 South 500 East
Vernal, Utah 84078
Phone: 789-1362

Henry Mountain Resource Area
P.O. Box 99
Hanksville, Utah 84734
Phone: 542-3461

Moab District Office
82 East Dogwood
P.O. Box 970
Moab, Utah 84532
Phone: 259-6111

Price River Resource Area
San Rafael Resource Area
900 North 700 East
P.O. Box AB
Price, Utah 84501

Grand Resource Area
Sand Flats Road
P.O. Box M
Moab, Utah 84532
Phone: 259-8193

State Parks

UTAH DIVISION OF PARKS AND RECREATION
1636 West North Temple
Salt Lake City, Utah 84116
Phone: 538-7220   1-800-284-2264
*State parks information
*Utah boating information
CENTRAL REGION OFFICE
1636 West North Temple
Salt Lake City, Utah 84116
Phone: 538-7337
STATE PARK CAMPGROUND RESERVATIONS:
Mistix   284
Toll-Free Phone: 1-800-322-2267
P.O. Box 680039
Park City, Utah 84068-0039

Deer Creek
P.O. Box 257
Midway, Utah 84049-0257

Rockport
P.O. Box 457
Peoa, Utah 84061-0457

Starvation
P.O. Box 584
Duchesne, Utah 84021-0584

Steinaker
Steinaker Lake 4335
Vernal, Utah 84078

Utah Lake
4400 West Center
Provo, Utah 84601-9715

Wasatch Mountain
P.O. Box 10
Midway, Utah 84049-0010

Yuba
P.O. Box 88
Levan, Utah 84639-0088

NORTHERN REGION OFFICE
1084 North Redwood Road
Salt Lake City, Utah 84116-1555
Phone: 533-5127

Bear Lake
P.O. Box 184
Garden City, Utah 84028-0184

East Canyon
P.O. Box 97
Morgan, Utah 84050-0097

Great Salt Lake
Saltair Beach
P.O. Box 323
Magna, Utah 84044-0323

Hyrum
405 West 300 South
Hyrum, Utah 84319-1547

Willard Bay
P.O. Box 319
Willard, Utah 84340-0319

SOUTHEAST REGION OFFICE
125 West 200 North
Moab, Utah 84532-2330
Phone: 259-8151

Dead Horse Point
P.O. Box 609
Moab, Utah 84532-0609

Goblin Valley
P.O. Box 93
Green River, Utah 84525-0093

Green River
P.O. Box 93
Green River, Utah 84525-0093

Huntington
P.O. Box 1343
Huntington, Utah 84528-1343

Palisade
P.O. Box H
Manti, Utah 84642-0076

Scofield
P.O. Box 166
Price, Utah 84501-0166

SOUTHWEST REGION OFFICE
P.O. Box 1079
Cedar City, Utah 84720-1079

Coral Pink Sand Dunes
P.O. Box 95
Kanab, Utah 84741-0095

Escalante Petrified Forest
P.O. Box 350
Escalante, Utah 84726-0350

Kodachrome Basin
P.O. Box 238
Cannonville, Utah 84718-0238

Minersville
P.O. Box 51
Beaver, Utah 84713-0051

Otter Creek
P.O. Box 43
Antimony, Utah 84712-0043

Snow Canyon
P.O. Box 140
Santa Clara, Utah 84765-0140

State park information, maps, brochures and other publications are available at both the Utah Travel Council and State Office of the Division of Parks and Recreation as well as the following visitor centers:

Anasazi, Boulder
Bear Lake, Garden City
Dead Horse Point near Moab
Edge of the Cedars, Blanding
Iron Mission, Cedar City
Pioneer Trail, Salt Lake City
Stagecoach Inn, Fairfield
Territorial Statehouse, Fillmore
Utah Field House of Natural History, Vernal
Wasatch Mountain, Midway

National Parks, Monuments, and Recreation Areas

Camping Information and Where to Write:

Arches National Park
c/o Canyonlands National Park
Moab, Utah 84532
Devils Garden Campground is located 18 miles north of the Visitor Center and has 54 total units.

Bryce Canyon National Park
Bryce Canyon, Utah 84717
North Campground is located just east of park headquarters and has 11 units. Sunset Campground is located two miles south of park headquarters and has 115 units.

Canyonlands National Park
Moab, Utah 84532
Squaw Flat Campground is located 35 miles west of U.S. 191 on Highway 211 and has 26 units. Willow Flat Campground is located 41 miles west off U.S. 191 on Highway 313.

Cedar Breaks National Monument
Box 749
Cedar City, Utah 84720
Point Supreme Campground is located two miles north of south entrance and has 30 units.

Capitol Reef National Park
Torrey, Utah 84775
Capitol Reef Campground is located 1.3 miles off Highway 24 and has 53 units. Cedar Mesa Campground is located 20 miles off Highway 24 and has five units.

Dinosaur National Monument
Box 210
Dinosaur, Colorado 81610
Green River Campground is located five miles east of Dinosaur Quarry and has 100 units. Rainbow Park is located 25 miles from Dinosaur Quarry and has four units. Split Mountain is located four miles east of the Dinosaur Quarry and has 35 units.

Flaming Gorge National Recreation Area
P.O. Box 278
Manila, Utah 84046
Campgrounds include at Antelope Flat 10.9 miles northwest off Highway 260 (122 units); Arch Dam Group 2.8 miles southwest off Highway 260 (200 units); Canyon Rim 15 miles southwest off Highway 44 (19 units); Cedar Springs 6.2 miles southwest off Highway 260 (23 units); Deer Run 5.8 miles southwest off Highway 260 (19 units); Dripping Springs three miles southeast (5 units); Firefighters Memorial 6.5 miles southwest off Highway 260 (94 units); Greendale 8.3 miles southwest off Highway 260 (7 units); Greens Lake 14.7 miles southwest off Highway 44 (19 units); Mustang Ridge four miles southwest off Highway 260 (73 units); Red Canyon 15.8 miles north off Highway 44 (eight units); Skull Creek 12.5 miles southwest off Highway 44 (17 units). All mileages figured from town of Dutch John.

Glen Canyon National Recreation Area
Box 1507
Page, Arizona 86040
Campgrounds include Bullfrog 70 miles south of Hanksville on Highway 276 with 86 units; Halls Grossing 95 miles southwest of Blanding on Highway 263 with 65 units, Hite 45 miles south of Hanksville on Highway 95 with six units, and Wahweap near Page, Arizona.

Golden Spike National Monument
P.O. Box L
Brigham City, Utah 84302
No Campground

Hovenweep National Monument
McElmo Route
Cortez, Colorado 81321
Square Ruin Campground is located 15 miles north of Aneth off Highway 262 and has 31 units.

Natural Bridges National Monument
c/o Canyonlands National Park
Moab, Utah 84532
Natural Bridges Campground is located four miles northwest off Highway 95 and has 13 units.

Pipe Springs National Monument
Moccasin, Arizona 86022
No Campground

Timpanogos Cave National Monument
Route 2, Box 200
American Fork, Utah 84003
No Campground

Zion National Park
Springdale, Utah 84767
Campgrounds include Lava Point 26 miles north of Virgin off Highway 9 with
four units; South near the south entrance to the park with 144 units and
Watchman near the south entrance with 229 units.

Visitor Information

Edge of the Cedars State Park
660 West 400 North
Blanding, Utah 84511
Phone: 678-2238

Bountiful Area Chamber of Commerce
145 North Main
Second Flour
Bountiful, Utah 84010
Phone: 295-6944

Brigham City Chamber of Commerce
6 North Main Street
Brigham City, Utah 84302
Phone 723-3931
Visitor Information Center on I-15

Bryce Canyon National Park
Visitor Center
Bryce Canyon, Utah 84717
Phone: 834-5322

Cedar City Chamber of Commerce
286 North Main
Cedar City, Utah 84720
Phone: 586-4484

Duchesne Chamber of Commerce
179 East Main
Duchesne, Utah 84021
Phone: 738-2501

Echo Information Center
I-80
Echo, Utah 84024
Phone: 336-2588

Visitor Information
Fairview Museum
Fairview, Utah 84629

Visitor Information
Territorial Statehouse State Park
Fillmore, Utah 84631

Green River Information Center
3rd Avenue and South River Blvd.
Green River, Utah 84525
Phone: 564-3325

Visitor Information
Hanksville, Utah 84734

Garfield County Information Center
Hatch, Utah 84735

Heber Information Center
Red Caboose on Main Street
Heber City, Utah 84032
Phone: 654-3666

Dinosaur National Monument
Visitor Center and Quarry
Jensen, Utah 84035
Phone: 789-2115

Visitor Information
Piute County Courthouse
Junction, Utah 84740

Kane County Visitor Center
48 South 100 East
Kanab, Utah 84741
Phone: 644-5033

Cache Chamber of Commerce
Logan, Utah 84321
Phone: 752-2161

Manila Chamber of Commerce
Manila, Utah 84046
Phone: 784-3737

Arches National Park Visitor Center
Moab, Utah 84532
Phone: 259-8161

Canyonlands National Park
Moab, Utah 84532
Phone: 259-7164

Grand County Travel Council
805 North Main Street
Moab, Utah 84532
Phone: 259-8825

Canyonlands National Park
Monticello, Utah 84535
Phone: 587-2737

San Juan County Visitor Center
117 South Main Street
Monticello, Utah 84535
Phone: 587-2231

Monument Valley Information Center
Monument Valley, Utah 84536

Little Sahara Recreation Area
Nephi, Utah 84648

Golden Spike Empire
Union Station
25th and Wall Avenue
Ogden, Utah 84402
Phone: 399-8288

Orem City Chamber of Commerce
56 North State
Orem, Utah 84057
Phone: 224-7000

Garfield County Information Center
Panguitch, Utah 84759

Park City Chamber Bureau
528 Main Street
Park City, Utah 84060
Phone: 649-6100

Carbon County Chamber of Commerce
Municipal Building
Price, Utah 84501
Phone: 637-2788

Provo City Chamber of Commerce
10 East 300 North
Provo, Utah 84601
Phone: 373-6770

Utah County Visitors Center
1425 South University Avenue
Provo, Utah 84601
Phone: 374-8687

Panoramaland
County Courthouse
Richfield, Utah 84701
Phone: 896-9222

Roosevelt Chamber of Commerce
332 South 200 East
Roosevelt, Utah 84066
Phone: 722-4598

Salt Lake Area Chamber of Commerce
19 East 200 South
Salt Lake City, Utah 84111
Phone: 364-3631

Salt Lake Valley Convention and Visitors Bureau
180 South West Temple
Salt Lake City, Utah 84101
Phone: 521-2822

Trolley Square Information Center
600 East 550 South
Salt Lake City, Utah 84102

Utah Travel Council
Council Hall/Capitol Hill
Salt Lake City, Utah 84114
Phone: 533-5681

Zion National Park Visitor Center
Springdale, Utah 84767
Phone: 772-3256

Springville Chamber of Commerce
175 South Main
Springville, Utah 84663
Phone: 489-4681

LDS Temple Visitor Center
450 South 300 East
St. George, Utah 84770
Phone: 673-5181

St. George Chamber of Commerce
97 East St. George Blvd.
St. George, Utah 84770
Phone: 628-1658

Visitor Information Center
I-70
Thompson, Utah 84540
Phone: 285-2234

Tooele Chamber of Commerce
90 North Main
Tooele, Utah 84074
Phone: 833-0690

Capitol Reef National Park
Visitor Center
Torrey, Utah 84775
Phone: 425-3871

Visitor Information Center
Natural History Museum
Vernal, Utah 84078
Phone: 789-4002

Vernal Chamber of Commerce
120 East Main Street
Vernal, Utah 84078
Phone: 789-1352

Reference Books

More detailed information can be obtained from the following publications which are available at most book stores throughout the state or by mail from Wasatch Publishers, Inc., 4647 Idlewild Road, Salt Lake City, Utah 84124.

The Hikers Guide to Utah
Hiking the Escalante
Wasatch Trails, Volumes 1 and 2
Utah Valley Trails
High Uinta Trails
Wasatch Tours
Canyon Country Hiking and Natural History
Canyon Country Off-Road Vehicle Trail Map, Island Area
Canyon Country Off-Road Vehicle Trail Map, Arches and LaSals Area
Canyon Country Off-Road Vehicle Trail Map, Canyon Rims and Needles
Canyon Country Camping
Canyon Country Geology
Canyon Country Paddles
Canyon Country Prehistoric Indians
Canyon Country Prehistoric Rock Art
Canyon Country Arches and Bridges
The Bicycle Tour Guide to Utah
Park City Trails
Utah Canyon Country
Utah Ski Country
Salt Lake Area Hiking Map
Provo Area Hiking Map
River Runners Guide to Utah
Utah, A Guide to the State
Utah Ghost Towns
Canyon Hiking Guide to the Colorado Plateau
Utah's Scenic San Rafael Swell
Hiking Utah's San Rafael Swell

Index

About the Author

There was a time in Tom Wharton's life when the thought of hiking, skiing or camping away from modern conveniences would have driven him into a basketball gymnasium for several days.

A wife who loved the outdoors, a chance to become the outdoor editor of *The Salt Lake Tribune* and four children whose idea of a great time is camping out in a slickrock desert changed all that.

Though he has traveled all over the world as a member of the Utah National Guard and the Outdoor Writers Association of America, Tom's favorite place to vacation is at home in Utah. As a high school sports writer and outdoor editor for *The Tribune*, he has explored nearly every road, hamlet and park in Utah. Though Tom has seen more than most, he knows there are enough places left to explore in Utah to last a lifetime.

Though he has been published in *Outdoor Life, Field and Stream* and *Fins and Feathers* magazines, *Utah! A Family Travel Guide* is Tom's first book. The work represents the culmination of a dream to bring families closer by exploring nature together.

About the Photographer

Dan Miller, whose photos appear in *Utah! A Family Travel Guide*, is a staff photographer for *The Salt Lake Tribune*. On one of his more recent assignments climbing peaks in the Flaming Gorge area, a Rocky Mountain Bighorn Sheep leapt in front of him. True to form, Dan kept snapping photos in spite of the fact that the bighorn sheep began talking to him.

"Dan Miller, I know you. You have two children, Rustee and Marci. You are also a photographer whose work has appeared in such diverse publications as *Solar Age* and *Utah Holiday*."

Dan tried in vain to interrupt.

"Stop! Wait!"

The bighorn continued. "Dan, you don't have to be sheepish with me and, by the way, why are you shooting landscapes again? I thought you were busy exploring the medium through innovative use of studio lighting, multi-exposure and large format techniques."

Dan started out, "Well, I was. I mean, I am, anyway how do you know my. . . ."

"How do I know your name? Isn't it obvious? We bighorns stay on top of things. We know that you have several gallery shows and awards to your credit, not to mention photographs in the permanent collection at the American Express Building that in no way resemble Karl Malden. It is a mystery to me why anyone would backpack, mountain climb, cross country ski and who knows what else to photograph."

Dan tried to interrupt from behind the camera, "But, but. . . ."

"Butt!" exclaimed the bighorn. "Why you're no more than a few feet from me, and if I were to butt you from this cliff, you'd never say cheese again."

Dan had had enough. He pulled the sleeping bag over his eyes.

"That's the last time I count sheep," he thought to himself as the full moon dropped behind the mountains.

About the Artist

"Where do you come from?" a friend recently asked artist Steve Baker.

"Well . . . I guess Utah," replied the artist, thinking of all the states he had lived in.

"What state do you call home?"

"Utaaaaaah!!!!"

Steve feels Utah is a nice place to call home, with its scenic beauty, majestic mountains, redrock cliffs, awe-inspiring canyons, vast deserts, clear blue lakes and wildlife.

As a child, Baker drew everything which inspired him. He drew his mother's pots and pans, doodads, lamps, flowers and, of course, Mom. Thirty-four years later, he's still drawing.

Steve attended Utah Technical College in Salt Lake where he studied graphic design. He is currently an artist for *The Salt Lake Tribune.*